D0522098

TISH
FOSTER
MANSELL
DENIM
Canon
Mobil
1

CAMEL
Labatt's

This edition produced
by Ted Smart for
The Book People
Guardian House
Borough Road
Godalming
Surrey GU7 2AE

Photography by Allsport UK
3 Greenlea Park, Prince George's Road
London SW19 2JD
Main contributors:
Pascal Rondeau and Mike Hewitt.
Other contributors:
Howard Boylan, Stephen Munday,
Jean-Marc Loubat, Bernard Asset.
Picture editor/researcher: John Bone

Production: Ted Smart
Design: Simon Verrall
Production Assistant: Seni Glaister

ISBN 1 85613 086 X

Manufactured in Spain.

MANSELL
World Champion

Text by
Terence O'Rorke

TED SMART

Silverstone *12 July, 1992. Britain's hero Nigel Mansell greets the crowd ecstatically after winning his most dominant Grand Prix, keeping the massive crowd cool with his champagne, and celebrating in a quieter fashion with wife, Rosanne.*

Foreword

It is the sign of a true sporting champion when you can come back from the pits of despair. When, after years of hard work and sacrifice, you have come so close to that coveted world title, only to have it taken away from you at the last hurdle. Many sportsman have folded under such bitter disappointment, finding it impossible to rid themselves of the seeds of doubt that are born from such an experience. They know better than anyone the levels of commitment that are required to perform at the highest level, and sometimes they are unable to put themselves through it all again.

But in Nigel Mansell, Britain has a sportsman of rare determination. A sportsman who has suffered more set-backs than most, but has still managed to pull through because of his exceptional self-belief. By winning the 1992-93 Formula One Driver's World Championship, Mansell has given us a unique insight into how to turn adversity into advantage; he has learnt from every moment of failure and taken stock of every piece of bad luck. Each experience has helped to make him even more dogged in his pursuit of sporting excellence.

Nigel Mansell's bad luck is legendary. During the 1985/86 Formula One season, he started living up to what most motor-racing experts had suspected for some time – that he was an exceptionally talented driver and, with the right car and back-up team, a potential world champion.

With only the Adelaide Grand Prix remaining, Mansell and his Williams Honda car were leading the Championship with a total of 72 points. There were a variety of permutations as to the outcome of the Championship, depending on the results in Adelaide. But the bottom line was that Mansell had to come third to guarantee himself the title. And with only eighteen laps of the season remaining, everything was going smoothly and according to plan. Despite a frequent change-over in the lead, Mansell had driven a sensible and controlled race. He was comfortable in third place, and looked all set to win the title.

(Top) Mansell waits patiently as his mechanics make final adjustments before shattering his own qualifying lap record by almost three seconds. (Above) Nigel works with his mechanics to improve even the tiniest details of his car.

But then disaster struck. His left rear-tyre blew at 150mph. In a matter of seconds, gone were his chances of securing third place and gone were his chances of winning the World Championship. What's more, arch-rival Alain Prost went on to win the race and take the title. Mansell had lost the championship in the cruellest of circumstances. It was typical of the luck he has experienced through-out his career and as he threatened to retire, few people imagined he would ever come so close again.

Lady-luck betrayed Mansell on that occasion, as it did when he came runner-up in 1987 and 1991. But during the 1992 Formula One season, he made sure there was little room for luck, as he went on to break record after record with the outstanding Williams-Renault team. With his near-total domination, Mansell dispelled all doubts about his temperament and ability, and proved once and for all that he deserves to be ranked alongside the greats of Formula One. This analysis of each of his races up to the Italian Grand Prix, where the championship was won, will show just how commanding he was in his drive for success. ■

1984

After a brief spell in Formula Ford, Nigel Mansell was spotted by Colin Chapman, who gave him his first opportunity to drive a formula one car. It was a test drive at Paul Ricard in 1979 and Mansell impressed sufficiently to be offered a full-time contract the following season. It had taken years of sacrifice and hardship, but he had finally made it.

By 1984 Mansell, still driving for Lotus-Renault, had established himself in the world of Formula One, and though he had yet to win a race, he had recorded some encouraging third and fourth places. But the season was not a great success for Mansell or Lotus. Instead, it was dominated by the McLarens of Niki Lauda and Alain Prost, who had won 12 of the 16 races. What's more, Mansell was continually clashing with Lotus' new team-manager, Peter Warr.

However, by this stage Mansell was starting to show real speed. In Monaco he qualified on the front row and even led the race for six laps, before spinning out in the rain, and during the Portuguese Grand Prix he also ran second for a while.

At the end of the season Mansell's contract with Lotus expired

1984 Championship Results

Country	Circuit	Driver	Manufacturer
Brazil	Rio de Janeiro	Prost	McLaren-TAG/Porsche
South Africa	Kyalami	Lauda	McLaren-TAG/Porsche
Belgium	Zolder	Alboreto	Ferrari
San Marino	Imola	Prost	McLaren-TAG/Porsche
France	Dijon-Prenois	Lauda	McLaren-TAG/Porsche
Monaco	Monte Carlo	Prost	McLaren-TAG/Porsche
Canada	Montreal	Piquet	Brabham-BMW
USA	Detroit	Piquet	Brabham-BMW
USA	Dallas	Rosberg	Williams-Honda
Britain	Brands Hatch	Lauda	McLaren-TAG/Porsche
Germany	Hockenheim	Prost	McLaren-TAG/Porsche
Austria	Osterreichring	Lauda	McLaren-TAG/Porsche
Netherlands	Zandvoort	Prost	McLaren-TAG/Porsche
Italy	Monza	Lauda	McLaren-TAG/Porsche
Europe	Nurburgring	Prost	McLaren-TAG/Porsche
Portugal	Estoril	Prost	McLaren-TAG/Porsche

Driver's Championship		Manufacturer's Championship	
Lauda	72 pts	McLaren-TAG/Porsche	143.5 pts
Prost	71.5 pts	Ferrari	57.5 pts
De Angelis	34 pts	Lotus-Renault	47 pts
Alboreto	30 pts	Brabham-BMW	38 pts

and Warr had no intentions of extending it. During his time with Lotus, Mansell had shown some flashes of brilliance, but hadn't necessarily appeared as a world champion in the making. His best was yet to come. ■

(Above) Nigel Mansell drives the John Player Special Lotus at Brands Hatch. By 1984 the fresh faced Englishman (above right) had led a Grand Prix, but the Lotus-Renault (right) was unable to provide him with his first win.

1985

When Lotus let Mansell go at the end of 1984, Frank Williams was quick to employ the services of the ever-improving English driver, and he was signed up to partner ex-World Champion, Keke Rosberg, in the Williams-Honda team.

In a more relaxed environment, it didn't take Mansell long to show what he was capable of and he was soon matching Rosberg for pace. As the season progressed the better Mansell became, and in the last seven races Mansell out-qualified Rosberg on five occasions.

In Belgium he finished second behind Ayrton Senna, and then came the moment he had been waiting most of his life for, his first Grand Prix win. And the venue could not have been more appropriate – the European Grand Prix at Brands Hatch.

A further victory in the South African Grand Prix and Mansell had justified the faith shown in him by Frank Williams. He finished equal fifth in the Drivers Championship, alongside his Finnish team-mate, and more importantly he established the Williams FW10 as a car to be reckoned with. Things were looking up for the following season. ■

(Top) The opening race of the season in Brazil saw a new team for Mansell (top right). The latest Williams (above and right) with the very powerful Honda engine was to provide Nigel with that first elusive win.

1985 Championship Results

Country	Circuit	Driver	Manufacturer
Brazil	Rio de Janeiro	Prost	McLaren-TAG/Porsche
Portugal	Estoril	Senna	Lotus-Renault
San Marino	Imola	De Angelis	Lotus-Renault
Monaco	Monte Carlo	Prost	McLaren-TAG/Porsche
Canada	Montreal	Alboreto	Ferrari
USA	Detroit	Rosberg	Williams-Honda
France	Paul Ricard	Piquet	Brabham-BMW
Britain	Silverstone	Prost	McLaren-TAG/Porsche
Germany	Nurburgring	Alboreto	Ferrari
Austria	Osterreichring	Prost	McLaren-TAG/Porsche
Netherlands	Zandvoort	Lauda	McLaren-TAG/Porsche
Italy	Monza	Prost	McLaren-TAG/Porsche
Belgium	Spa-Francorchamps	Senna	Lotus-Renault
Europe	Brands Hatch	Mansell	Williams-Honda
South Africa	Kyalami	Mansell	Williams-Honda
Australia	Adelaide	Rosberg	Williams-Honda

Driver's Championship		Manufacturer's Championship	
Prost	73 pts	McLaren-TAG Porsche	90 pts
Alboreto	53 pts	Ferrari	82 pts
Rosberg	40 pts	Williams-Honda	71 pts
Senna	38 pts	Brabham-BMW	26 pts

October 6th 1985 saw Nigel Mansell's first win at Brands Hatch. "Red Five" storming to victory in front of a massive partisan crowd. The race saw two first-time winners, with Nigel taking his first win and his friend Alain Prost (right) his first World Championship.

1986

When Keke Rosberg decided to spend his last season in Formula One driving for McLaren, Nelson Piquet was brought in to partner Mansell in the Williams team. Piquet had been with Brabham for seven years, and was regarded by some observers as the best driver around.

The Williams team were looking strong favourites for the forthcoming season; they had two of the most skillful drivers in the world, and, after some successful pre-season testing, their cars were looking more promising than ever.

But it was also obvious that their two drivers were not going to hit it off. Piquet's confidence irritated his team-mate, and Mansell was also somewhat upset by the fact that the Brazilian driver received the lion's share of support from the team.

A further blow was dealt when team-owner Frank Williams was paralysed after suffering severe injuries in a car crash. The team, however, was determined to pull together, and they got just the result they needed when Piquet won the first race of the season on his home track.

Mansell managed second place in Spain and a fourth in Monaco before tragedy struck once more – Elio De Angelis, Mansell's friend and Lotus team-mate of four years died during testing at Paul Ricard. Mansell responded in the best possible way – he won in Belgium, dedicating the victory to Elio, and then again at Brands Hatch, after an exhilarating battle with Piquet.

(Facing page) With two wins under his belt, Nigel went confidently into 1986 proving quicker than ever before (top) with his Williams-Honda FW11. Nigel also found for the first time a committed team (bottom), backing him up, off the track, in the garage and in the pit lane.

(This page) By mid-season Mansell was a strong championship contender. At Brands Hatch in July he scorched to victory (above) in front of a delighted British crowd (below). At the mid-point of the season, the jubilant Briton (right) found himself leading the World Championship tables for the first time.

1986

The tension continued between the two drivers, as they both vied for the attentions of the Williams designers and engineers. After a few mediocre results Mansell put himself back in the running after a sensational drive in Portugal. He now had a ten point lead in the World Championship with two rounds to go.

At the Mexican Grand Prix, Mansell needed to finish in front of Piquet (second in the championship), and Prost (lying third), to secure the title. He managed to qualify on the second row, but as the lights turned green, he failed to engage gear and was left on the grid. Berger won the race, Prost took second and Piquet fourth. Mansell failed to gain any points, but going into the final race in Adelaide he still maintained a six point lead over Prost and a seven point lead over his team-mate.

October 26th 1986, the date of the Adelaide Grand Prix, will forever be etched in the memory of Nigel Mansell. After fifteen gruelling races, he knew exactly what was required of him on the day – third place would give him the championship. And qualifying could not have gone better, as he kept a cool head to record the fastest lap and take pole position.

With three-quarters of the race gone, things were going smoothly, Mansell had kept out of trouble and was comfortable in third place – he even allowed several of his rivals through just so he could maintain a steady pace in third. But on lap 63, the Williams team got the first, and only, indication that

(Facing page and above) Honda found reliability in their 1.5 litre turbo engine complemented by the Williams chassis. The fastest driver of the field, Nigel's season was plagued by bad luck and retirements (below). Despite his many victories, his misfortune allowed rivals Alain Prost and Nelson Piquet (right) to stay in contention for the world title.

1986

HONDA
GOODYEAR
DENIM
Canon
Mobil
1
BOSS
Isle of Man
ICI
DENIM
PMG
Canon
calma
Tactel
Mobil
Canon
DENIM
Mobil
HONDA
Tactel
HONDA
Mobil
GOODYEAR
Canon

trouble lay ahead. Mansell's ex-team-mate, Keke Rosberg, now driving for McLaren, was forced to retire with tyre trouble, and as Mansell had an ample lead over the fourth placed car, the team decided to call him for a tyre change.

Unfortunately they never got the chance. On lap 64 Mansell's left tyre exploded and the Englishman had to count on all his driving ability to keep the car straight and avoid crashing at 150 mph.

He was out of the race, and what's more, the incident persuaded Piquet to pit for a tyre change. This gave Alain Prost the lead, the race and the championship.

Mansell finished the season in second place two points behind Prost. The Williams team won the Constructor's Championship ahead of McLaren. Mansell had outdriven his team-mate so the season was by no means a disaster for Mansell and the Williams team. But nothing could make up for the disappointment of Adelaide. ■

(Facing page) The penultimate race at Mexico saw more drama for Mansell while leading the Championship, when he forgot to engage first gear at the start. 18th on lap one, Nigel drove superbly to 5th, but rivals Prost (above) and Piquet finished ahead of him.

The Championship would be decided in Australia (right). Mansell led Prost early on, but with a mere eighteen laps to go, the dream ended with a tyre exploding, leaving a bitterly disappointed Nigel (below right) walking back to the pits as a runner-up in the Championship.

1986 Championship Results

Country	Circuit	Driver	Manufacturer
Brazil	Rio de Janeiro	Piquet	Williams-Honda
Spain	Jerez de la Frontera	Senna	Lotus-Renault
San Marino	Imola	Prost	McLaren-TAG/Porsche
Monaco	Monte Carlo	Prost	McLaren-TAG/Porsche
Belgium	Spa-Francorchamps	Mansell	Williams-Honda
Canada	Montreal	Mansell	Williams-Honda
USA	Detroit	Senna	Lotus-Renault
France	Paul Ricard	Mansell	Williams-Honda
Britain	Brands Hatch	Mansell	Williams-Honda
Germany	Hockenheim	Piquet	Williams-Honda
Hungary	Hungaroring	Piquet	Williams-Honda
Austria	Osterreichring	Prost	McLaren-TAG/Porsche
Italy	Monza	Piquet	Williams-Honda
Portugal	Estoril	Mansell	Williams-Honda
Mexico	Mexico City	Berger	Benetton-BMW
Australia	Adelaide	Prost	McLaren-TAG/Porsche

Driver's Championship

Prost	72 pts
Mansell	70 pts
Piquet	69 pts
Senna	55 pts

Manufacturer's Championship

Williams-Honda	141 pts
McLaren-TAG/Porsche	96 pts
Lotus-Renault	58 pts
Ferrari	37 pts

1987

To Nigel Mansell's credit, he came back from the bitter disappointments of '86 with renewed enthusiasm. He knew that it was not his driving which had let him down the season before and he was keener than ever to prove he was the world number 1.

Again his main rival was also his team-mate, Nelson Piquet, and if anybody thought that time would heal the rift between the two drivers, then they couldn't have been more wrong. If anything, their relationship had deteriorated even more!

The FW11B was certainly the car of the moment and it was clear the Championship was going to go to one of the two Williams drivers. Mansell was in a dominant mood throughout the season, winning no fewer than six races. His victory over Piquet in the British Grand Prix was one of the most sensational of his career, as he fought back from a 28 second deficit, with only 29 laps to go.

But Piquet was also driving exceptionally well, and although he was only first to the chequered flag on two occasions during the season, his consistency was second to none. He came second seven times and scored points in 12 of the 16 rounds.

The Mexican Grand Prix provided another thrilling race and another chapter in the worsening relations between the two drivers. It was won by the Englishman, but not before the two of them treated the crowds to a right old ding-dong in the second part of the race.

In the post-race press conference, Mansell accused Piquet of unprofessional tactics while the Brazilian accused Mansell of talking "bullshit". Those who observed the events in Mexico could clearly see that their relationship had reached the point of no return!

With only Japan and Adelaide to go, Mansell was 12 points adrift of his team-mate and needed a victory in both races. But an accident in qualifying at Suzuka put paid to these designs. He suffered a crushed vertebrae and was forced to end his season early. His challenge had once again ended on a sour note, and with his dissatisfaction at Williams it was looking more and more likely that his Grand Prix days were over. ■

A blisteringly hot July saw another thrilling British Grand Prix (top and bottom). Mansell recovering from a pit-stop took the lead from team-mate Piquet with 3 laps to go, winning one of the best races in his career to the crowds delight.

1987

Above: Nigel Mansell battled all year, scoring an impressive six victories (right) compared to Nelson Piquet's three. Reliability helped Piquet keep his points score above Nigel's. With Mansell relentlessly persuing Piquet's title bid, an accident during practice for the Japanese Grand Prix (below) finally ended his championship hopes. Runner-up again.

1987 Championship Results

Country	Circuit	Driver	Manufacturer
Brazil	Rio De Janeiro	Prost	McLaren-TAG/Porsche
San Marino	Imola	Mansell	Williams-Honda
Belgium	Spa-Francorchamps	Prost	McLaren-TAG/Porsche
Monaco	Monte Carlo	Senna	Lotus-Honda
USA	Detroit	Senna	Lotus-Honda
France	Paul Ricard	Mansell	Williams-Honda
Britain	Silverstone	Mansell	Williams-Honda
Germany	Hockenheim	Piquet	Williams-Honda
Hungary	Hungaroring	Piquet	Williams-Honda
Austria	Osterreichring	Mansell	Williams-Honda
Italy	Monza	Piquet	Williams-Honda
Portugal	Estoril	Prost	McLaren-TAG/Porsche
Spain	Jerez de la Frontera	Mansell	Williams-Honda
Mexico	Mexico City	Mansell	Williams-Honda
Japan	Suzuka	Berger	Ferrari
Australia	Adelaide	Berger	Ferrari

Driver's Championship		Manufacturer's Championship	
Piquet	73 pts	Williams-Honda	137 pts
Mansell	61 pts	McLaren-TAG/Porsche	76 pts
Senna	57 pts	Lotus-Honda	64 pts
Prost	46 pts	Ferrari	53 pts

1988

Mansell came close to retiring at the end of the '87 season, but in the end he opted to stay in Formula One and stay with Williams, for the time being. He was joined by Italian Riccardo Patrese and was finally given the number one spot he deserved.

However, Williams' contract with Honda had expired, and they had to rely on the normally aspirated Judd engines. But despite a few impressive drives by Mansell, including a second at Silverstone, it became more and more obvious that the Judd's could not cope with the greater power of the turbos.

By this stage Mansell's thoughts were already elsewhere. In July of that year he signed a contract to drive for Ferrari in 1989, partnering Gerhard Berger. He needed a change and what could be better than joining the hallowed ranks of the famous Italian team? ■

Above: The new Williams FW12 chassis featuring an abortive active suspension coupled with a loss of Honda engines, left Nigel out of contention for 1988. Despite the finest work from the whole team, only two finishes were to go Nigel's way, undoubtedly the best of these was his superb second at the British Grand Prix at Silverstone. However, more success off-track at the Australian Open (below) saw a fine performance from expert golfer Nigel.

1988 Championship Results

Country	Circuit	Driver	Manufacturer
Brazil	Rio de Janeiro	Prost	McLaren-Honda
San Marino	Imola	Senna	McLaren-Honda
Monaco	Monte Carlo	Prost	McLaren-Honda
Mexico	Mexico City	Prost	McLaren-Honda
Canada	Montreal	Senna	McLaren-Honda
USA	Detroit	Senna	McLaren-Honda
France	Paul Ricard	Prost	McLaren-Honda
Britain	Silverstone	Senna	McLaren-Honda
Germany	Hockenheim	Senna	McLaren-Honda
Hungary	Hungaroring	Senna	McLaren-Honda
Belgium	Spa-Francorchamps	Senna	McLaren-Honda
Italy	Monza	Berger	Ferrari
Portugal	Estoril	Prost	McLaren-Honda
Spain	Jerez de la Frontera	Prost	McLaren-Honda
Japan	Suzuka	Senna	McLaren-Honda
Australia	Adelaide	Prost	McLaren-Honda

Driver's Championship		Manufacturer's Championship	
Senna	90 pts	McLaren-Honda	199 pts
Prost	87 pts	Ferrari	65 pts
Berger	41 pts	Benetton-Ford	39 pts
Boutsen	27 pts	Arrows-Megatron	23 pts

1989

At the beginning of 1989 Mansell was in a relaxed mood and looking forward to the season ahead. He has often been accused of being an awkward customer to work with and, as he began his spell with the Italian team, he was determined to change this opinion people had of him. And it didn't take him long to win the hearts of the fanatical Italian fans, the "tifosi", despite the fact that his John Barnard designed Ferrari 640 car had gear-box problems.

Going into the first race of the season, in Brazil, Mansell did not rate his chances very high. He could only qualify in sixth place, and during the warm-up he could only manage one lap. But somehow the car performed when it mattered and Mansell roared home to a totally unexpected victory.

All of a sudden Mansell was a national hero in Italy. The "tifosi" nicknamed him "Il Leone", the lion, for his courageous and skillful driving. However, the honeymoon period did not last long and any chance he had of challenging the McLarens disappeared when his gearbox failed him in three consecutive races.

But the problem was gradually sorted out and Mansell put in a series of good performances in the next five races, including an inspired drive in Hungary. Though he could only qualify in 12th position, he managed to weave his way through the field to take the chequered flag 26 seconds clear of Ayrton Senna's McLaren.

Though he managed a 3rd place in Belgium the rest of the season was a disaster. His car let him down on two more occasions, and then disqualified in Portugal. He was banned from driving in Spain, as a result of the controversial disqualification, and an accident in Adelaide forced him to retire.

For Nigel Mansell it was a season of highs and lows; he finished fourth in the Driver's Championship, while Ferrari came third in the constructor's Championship. He had certainly given the Italians something to cheer, but without a reliable car there was little more he could do. ■

1989 Championship Results

Country	Circuit	Driver	Manufacturer
Brazil	Rio de Janeiro	Mansell	Ferrari
San Marino	Imola	Senna	McLaren-Honda
Monaco	Monte Carlo	Senna	McLaren-Honda
Mexico	Mexico City	Senna	McLaren-Honda
USA	Arizona	Prost	Williams-Renault
France	Paul Ricard	Prost	Williams-Renault
Britain	Silverstone	Prost	Williams-Renault
Germany	Hockenheim	Senna	McLaren-Honda
Hungary	Hungaroring	Mansell	Ferrari
Belgium	Spa-Francorchamps	Senna	McLaren-Honda
Italy	Monza	Prost	McLaren-Honda
Portugal	Estoril	Berger	Ferrari
Spain	Jerez de la Frontera	Senna	McLaren-Honda
Japan	Suzuka	Nannini	Benetton-Ford
Australia	Adelaide	Boutsen	Williams-Renault

Driver's Championship		Manufacturer's Championship	
Prost	76 pts	McLaren-Honda	141 pts
Senna	60 pts	Williams-Renault	77 pts
Patrese	40 pts	Ferrari	59 pts
Mansell	38 pts	Benetton-Ford	39 pts

(Clockwise from top left): A switch to the famous Ferrari team in 1989 saw Nigel winning the hearts of all Italy when he won the first race of the season at Jacarepagua, Brazil, against all expectations. On the pace all year, reliability was not the strong point, only one other win was to come. A quite superb race saw Nigel win from 12th on the grid, pulling of a stupefying passing manoeuvre over Ayrton Senna for the lead on one of the hardest circuits of them all.

1990

(Top left) An Englishman Abroad – Nigel continued with Ferrari in 1990 with new team-mate Alain Prost (below). Nigel Mansell's aggressive racing style adding to the colour and spectacle of Monaco (above).

Mansell was hoping for better things from his car in 1990, but once again he was left disappointed. He only managed six finishes in the sixteen rounds of the Championship, and with less than half the season gone, his frustration had manifested itself to such a degree that he announced he was to retire at the end of the year.

At the beginning of the season he was joined by Alain Prost, and had therefore lost his 'No. 1' status. The two drivers decided to share the spare car and publicly declared their admiration for each other. Mansell wasn't best pleased with the decision, but as long as he received the back-up he needed and deserved then he saw no reason why they couldn't drive together.

But the cordial relations did not last long. Prost appeared to have the more reliable car and this wrangled with Mansell. Time and time again he demanded more from the team, only to find himself on the receiving end of a problematic gearbox or faulty engine. When he did manage to finish he gained good points – he had two second places, a third, a fourth and a victory in Portugal.

By the end of the season, the Mansell retirement saga had taken another twist. Frank Williams visited him at his home on the Isle of Man to try and entice him back into the Williams team, and as Mansell says, "I demanded the impossible and got it." He was back with his old team, and more importantly, he had the No. 1 spot he so desired. ■

1990

1990 Championship Results

Country	Circuit	Driver	Manufacturer
USA	Phoenix	Senna	McLaren-Honda
Brazil	Sao Paulo	Prost	Ferrari
San Marino	Imola	Patrese	Williams-Renault
Monaco	Monte Carlo	Senna	McLaren-Honda
Canada	Montreal	Senna	McLaren-Honda
Mexico	Mexico City	Prost	Ferrari
France	Paul Ricard	Prost	Ferrari
Britain	Silverstone	Prost	Ferrari
Germany	Hockenheim	Senna	McLaren-Honda
Hungary	Hungaroring	Boutsen	Williams-Renault
Belgium	Spa-Francorchamps	Senna	McLaren-Honda
Italy	Monza	Senna	McLaren-Honda
Portugal	Estoril	Mansell	Ferrari
Spain	Jerez	Prost	Ferrari
Japan	Suzuka	Piquet	Benetton-Ford
Australia	Adelaide	Piquet	Benetton-Ford

Driver's Championship		Manufacturer's Championship	
Senna	78 pts	McLaren-Honda	121 pts
Prost	71 pts	Ferrari	110 pts
Piquet	43 pts	Benetton-Ford	71 pts
Berger	43 pts	Williams-Renault	57 pts

(Above) Fast all season, Mansell's car did not have the reliability of Prost's. He led several races, such as the Japanese and British Grand Prix (left), in dominant form, and was always found racing hard (below) only to let down by the car.

1991

During the winter break, Williams' chief designer, Patrick Head, had been working hard on a semi-automatic gear-box in an effort to give Mansell, and his team-mate Riccardo Patrese, the car to challenge the dominance of the McLaren-Hondas. However, there hadn't been enough time to properly test the new technology and in the first two rounds Mansell was once again plagued by an unreliable car.

Ayrton Senna set a new Formula One record by winning the first four Grand Prix races of the season and it looked like the Brazilian driver was going to run away with The Championship once again. However, there had been promising signs from the new FW14, and when it was on-song it looked extremely good.

Senna was quick to notice this, and Mansell's season took a distinct turn for the better after the first three rounds. He finished

Lured back from 'retirement', Nigel returned to Williams for 1991 (top). The early season showed tremendous speed from the Renault V10 (right) but the new semi-automatic gearbox was unreliable (bottom right).

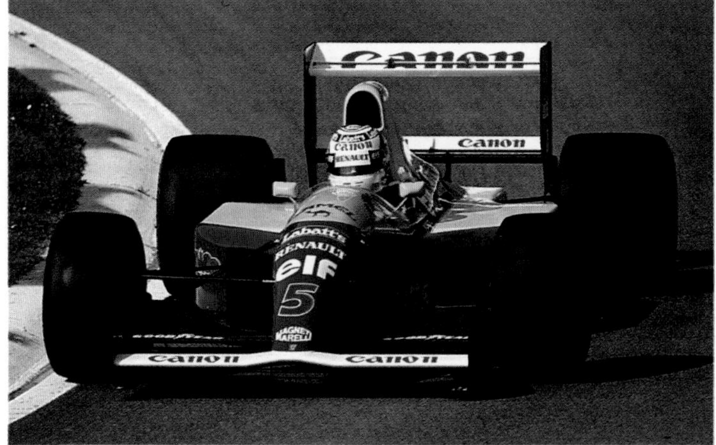

1991

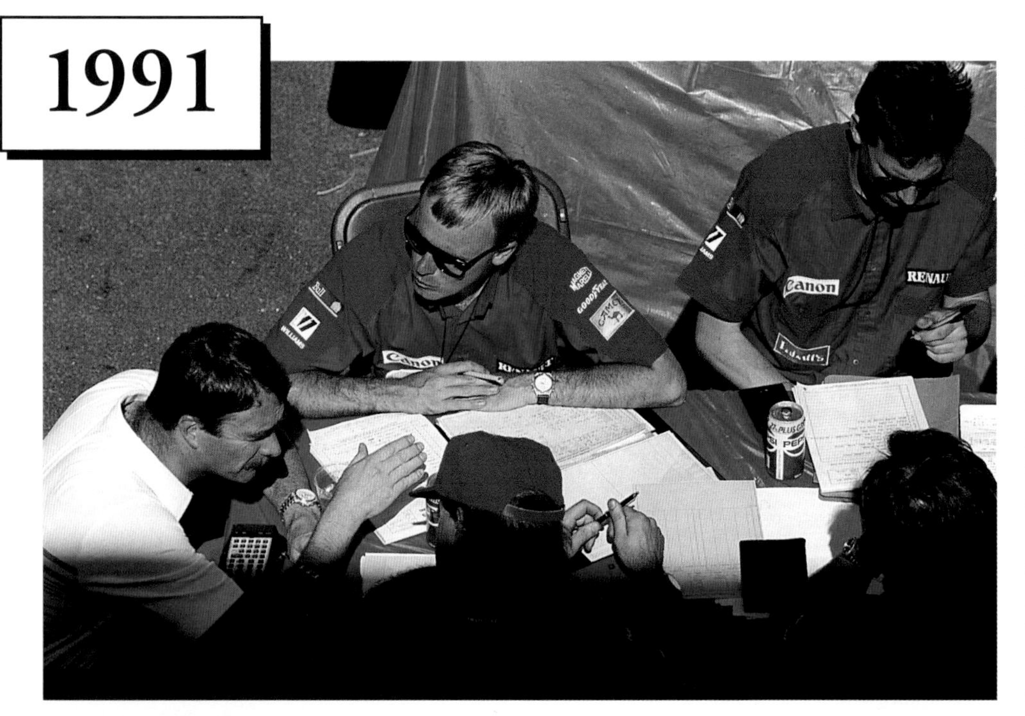

second to Senna in Monaco, and showed impressive form in Montreal as he led going into the final lap. Carelessness prevented him from winning on that occasion – as he waved to the crowd he failed to engage the correct gear and stalled the car – but he then went on to record a hat-trick of victories at Paul Ricard, Silverstone and Hockenheim.

The FW14 was now being tipped as the car to knock the McLaren's off the top spot and Mansell the driver to take over from Senna. With seven rounds still to go Mansell was a mere eight points behind the Brazilian and looked set to over-take his haul of points.

But Senna hit back in Hungary with a masterful display of controlled driving, keeping his line perfectly throughout the whole race and preventing the more powerful Williams from passing. Mansell still managed to take second place, but rather than making up some of the lee way, he found himself a further four points adrift.

At least the positions were reversed in Monza where Mansell finished first to Senna's second, and with the English driver

(Top and left) The team looking towards the Championship, Nigel won three races in a row before his stunning Spanish victory (below). (Facing page) Grabbing the lead from Senna in the most breathtaking manoeuvre of his career.

Marlboro
Canon
RENAULT
5

1991

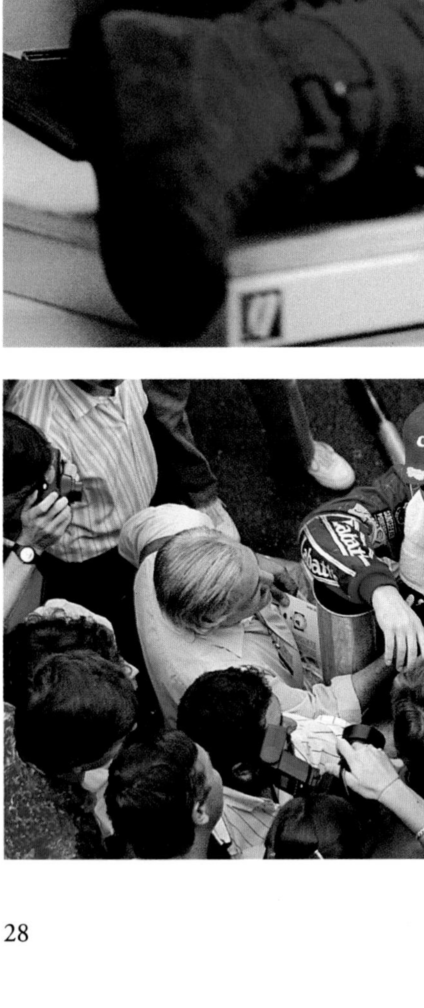

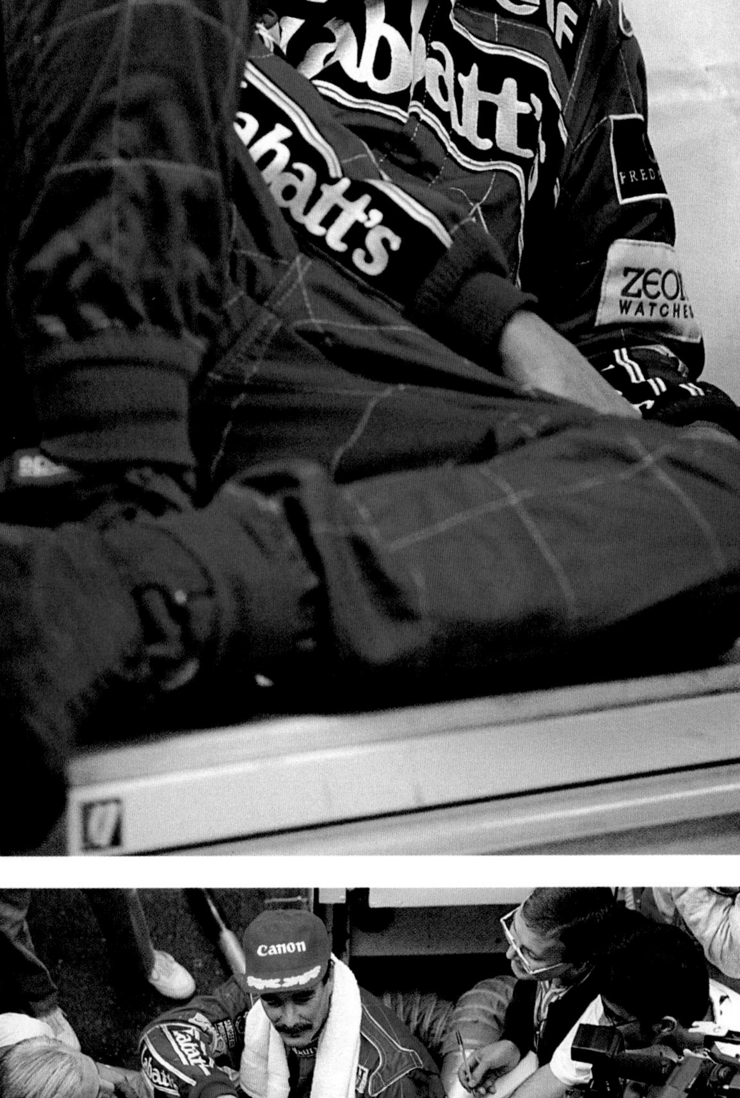

leading after 30 laps in Estoril he looked set to reduce the margin still further. But then disaster struck; as Mansell left the pits after a tyre change, his back-right tyre came away from the car. Another one was quickly attached, but it was in contravention of Formula One's laws as Mansell's FW14 now lay in the fast lane of the pits. Twenty laps on Mansell was disqualified, Senna took second place behind Patrese and the Championship was practically his.

A childish slanging match between Mansell and Senna kept the news hounds occupied prior to the Spanish Grand Prix, where Mansell took the chequered flag to

give himself an outside chance of the title. However, the Williams driver spun-off at Suzuka as he tried to press the McLarens and Senna was Champion for the third time in his career.

It was a season of 'ifs and buts' for Nigel Mansell, but one thing was for sure – the Williams drivers now had a car which could not only compete with the best that McLaren had to offer, but also beat them for speed and power.

If there was a lesson to be learnt from the four year dominance of the McLaren team, it was that reliability was the name of the game. It was no good having the fastest car in Formula One if it could only perform to its maximum for fifty per cent of the season. The Williams team knew they had the car to win the world title and as they readied themselves for an intense period of testing over the winter months, Mansell was looking forward to 1992 with an air of confidence. ■

Nigel (top left) went to Silverstone as firm favourite and did not disappoint his many admirers (left) in a brilliant show of speed and aggression (above). The highlight of the day (right) was when Ayrton Senna retired on the last lap and Nigel gave him a lift back to the pits before celebrating in grand style.

1991

In Japan Nigel (left) contemplates lost dreams; whilst chasing title rival Senna, he crashes out (below) ending his Championship dream. Australia finished the season badly, Nigel spinning in appalling conditions (above).

1991 Championship Results

Country	Circuit	Driver	Manufacturer
USA	Phoenix	Senna	McLaren-Honda
Brazil	Interlagos	Senna	McLaren-Honda
San Marino	Imola	Senna	McLaren-Honda
Monaco	Monte Carlo	Senna	McLaren-Honda
Canada	Montreal	Piquet	Benetton-Ford
Mexico	Mexico City	Patrese	Williams-Renault
France	Magny-Cours	Mansell	Williams-Renault
Britain	Silverstone	Mansell	Williams-Renault
Germany	Hockenheim	Mansell	Williams-Renault
Hungary	Hungaroring	Senna	McLaren-Honda
Belgium	Spa-Francorchamps	Senna	McLaren-Honda
Italy	Monza	Mansell	Williams-Renault
Portugal	Estoril	Patrese	Williams-Renault
Spain	Circuit de Catalunya	Mansell	Williams-Renault
Japan	Suzuka	Berger	McLaren-Honda
Australia	Adelaide	Senna	McLaren-Honda

Driver's Championship	
Senna	96 pts
Mansell	72 pts
Patrese	53 pts
Berger	43 pts

Manufacturer's Championship	
McLaren-Honda	139 pts
Williams-Renault	125 pts
Ferrari	55.5 pts
Benetton-Ford	38.5 pts

1992

Estoril *(This page) The Estoril testing saw a rejuvenated Nigel Mansell appear lighter, fitter and more motivated than ever before in order to win that elusive Championship, after wintering at his new Florida home.*

(Facing page) The Williams FW14 featured a new active suspension system, developed by Patrick Head, and superb aerodynamics from Adrian Newey, which, Mansell reckoned, saved the car a second per lap.

Estoril Test

During the 1991 season, Nigel Mansell and the Williams team conceded 30 points to arch-rivals Ayrton Senna and McLaren. After the first three rounds of the championship, Senna had amassed maximum points, while Mansell still had to get off the mark. This is not the sort of advantage you give to a driver like Senna or a team like McLaren if you want to entertain realistic designs on winning the Championship.

There were, however, reasons for their initial lack of success. They took a gamble introducing the new FW14, and its semi-automatic gearbox, when they did, as they hadn't had sufficient time to test it. But it was a risk they had to take to stand any chance of challenging the McLarens, and, as the season wore on, it became more and more apparent that the risk was worth taking.

The Williams team were determined to get off to a good start and avoid the problems they had encountered the previous year. The success of the McLaren's had brought it home that you need to score points in nearly every round of the Championship to stand a good chance of the title. It was all about consistency, and to achieve this they had to be more prepared than ever.

The two Williams drivers, with the assistance of test driver Damon Hill, therefore tested the new car over mile upon mile of the European circuits. It was still a risk introducing the car and its new active suspension, but at least they were confident in their own minds that they had done as much as was possible in preparation.

Nigel Mansell was also busy preparing himself physically for the gruelling months ahead. From his new home in Clearwater, Florida, he made sure that he was the fittest he had ever been for the start of a season. The warm climate enabled him to pursue a more rigourous fitness programme, and as a result he was several pounds lighter than in previous seasons.

Spending the winter in Florida also helped Mansell ready himself mentally. He could not only lead a more normal life out of the spotlight, but also devote more time to his wife Roseanne, and children Chloe, Leo and Greg. Those close to him noticed that he was more relaxed and composed than he had been for a long time, and this gave him renewed confidence for the season ahead.

Mansell and the Williams team had done their homework. The months of practice had gone well and they were as prepared as they could possibly be. They knew they were capable of winning both the Driver's and the Constructor's Championships and were keener than ever to get the ball rolling. ■

1992

The South African Grand Prix

In 1991, Nigel Mansell came runner-up in the World Championship for the third time in his career. He was, therefore, keener than ever to put in a good performance in the first Grand Prix of the season. The Williams team had worked hard on the car over the winter months, and from his new home in Clearwater, Florida, Mansell made sure he was fitter than he had ever been for the beginning of a championship.

Mansell has generally had inauspicious starts to the season, but at South Africa's revamped Kayalami track, he was determined to get off to a flyer, and what a start it proved to be. He was comfortably the fastest in practice, and though he spun off the track in the final session and was forced to use the spare car, he took pole position with nearly a second in hand.

It was the position he wanted and needed, as it was vital for him to get to the front in order to build a lead. With South Africa's sporting isolation, it was seven years since their last Grand Prix (which Mansell had won), and the new circuit at Kayalami was proving very different from the old one. As Mansell pointed out after his practice session, "The track is incredibly demanding. The only thing I would like there to be is one long straight, somewhere for overtaking, but even though I am saying that, it is fabulous."

The McLaren's of Ayrton Senna and Gerhard Berger qualified second and third respectively, with Mansell's Williams teammate Ricardo Patrese fourth, having experienced troubles with his gear box earlier in the session.

Rain was forecast for the day of the race, but in the event it remained dry with temperatures slightly down on the previous few days. There was also a slight problem with Mansell's drive-car; an electrical fault in the gear change had bothered the team during practice and they therefore decided to play safe and go with the spare. They worked through the night on the T-car, and did such a fantastic job that once again Mansell was comfortably the fastest during warm-up.

The start promised to be a race within a race, and it turned out to be sensational. But it was not Senna who threatened Mansell, rather his team-mate Patrese – a driver not renowned for his starts. This time, however, he came out fast, and as he squeezed between the two McLarens, it looked as if he might even overtake Mansell coming into the first corner.

Bur Mansell held on. He had got the start he wanted and from there on he drove a flawless race, gradually building up a comfortable lead. After 11 laps he was 10 seconds ahead of the second-placed Patrese, and 22 seconds ahead after 26 laps. Meanwhile Patrese had taken an 8 second lead over Senna, who appeared to be content with third place.

However, as the 50 lap mark approached, Senna began to close the gap on Patrese, and at one stage he was only a couple of seconds behind. He knew he wouldn't be able to overtake the Williams-Renault car, and was therefore relying on him either making a mistake or being held up by the back-runners. But Patrese was up to the task. He kept his cool under the pressure and made it a one-two for the Williams team, with Senna taking third.

Nigel Mansell had got the ten points he so desperately wanted, and what's more, over the four days he had hardly put a foot wrong. During the race he led from the start and finished with over twenty seconds to spare. The Williams-Renault team had set the pace for the rest of the Championship and were looking every bit as dominant as McLarens had done the season before. ■

The South African Grand Prix

Starting as he meant to go on, Nigel was fastest in each qualifying session, the race warm-up and the race itself. He took pole position track record and won by 25 seconds from team-mate Riccardo Patrese. Ayrton Senna was even further back, claiming that nobody would beat the Williams team,especially Nigel, in '92.

YEL
Canon

The South African Grand Prix – Kyalami.

The 1992 Formula One World Championship bursts into life with Mansell snatching the lead into the first turn.

CAMEL
Mobil 1
YELLOW PAGES
YELLOW PAGES
OFFICIAL SPONSOR
SOUTH AFRICAN
GRAND PRIX

South African Grand Prix Results

1 March • 72 laps, 191.727 miles

Starting Positions

1	N Mansell	2	A Senna
3	G Berger	4	R Patrese
5	J Alesi	6	M Schumacher
7	K Wendlinger	8	M Brundle
9	I Capelli	10	A De Cesaris

Finishing Positions and points

1	N Mansell	GB	Williams-Renault	10
2	R Patrese	France	Williams-Renault	6
3	A Senna	Brazil	McLaren-Honda	4
4	Schumacher	Germany	Benetton-Ford	3
5	G Berger	Austria	McLaren-Honda	2
6	J Herbert	GB	Lotus-Ford	1

1992 Driver's Championship to date and points

1	N Mansell	10	2	R Patrese	6
3	A Senna	4	4	M Schumacher	3
5	G Berger	2	6	J Herbert	1

1992 Constructor's Championship to date and points

1	Williams-Renault	16
2	McLaren-Honda	6
3	Benetton-Ford	3
4	Lotus-Ford	1

Fastest Lap

Mansell 1:17.578s (123.576 mph)

The South African Grand Prix

(Top, far left and left) Michael Schumacher and Johnny Herbert, two of the fastest and youngest rising stars in Formula One. (Top right) Mansell crushes the opposition, team-mate Riccardo Patrese (above) the only driver to be anywhere near Nigel's times. (Main picture) Nigel brings the crowd to their feet in a dominant display of Williams-Renault superiority, leaving him unchallenged from lights to flag as he starts his bid for the 1992 World Championship.

CAMEL
Labatt's
Bull

Nigel Mansell & Williams FW14B

Man and machine, the winning combination at Kyalami.

1992

The South African Grand Prix

Nigel Mansell streaks across the line for his first win of the year with team-mate Riccardo Patrese following him in second place.

1992

The Mexican Grand Prix

With their one-two victory in South Africa, the Williams team was justifiably confident during the run-up to the Mexican Grand Prix, held at the infamous Autodromo Hermanos Rodriguez.

Built on the bed of a dry lake, the circuit is one of the great race tracks of the world. It has fast corners, some long, overtaking straights, and the outstanding Peraltada curve – a 180 degree bend, with an alarming number of bumps. Mexican officials had reduced some of the banking and re-laid some of its surface in time for the 1992 Grand Prix, but the corner was still extremely dangerous.

In the early practice sessions Nigel Mansell again dominated the lap times, though Michael Schumacher in his Benetton Ford was having a terrific day. Ayrton Senna, who had crashed at the Peraltada in 1991, again lost control after hitting a bump in the esses. He was taken to hospital with severe bruising, but to the relief of everyone, returned to the track the following day.

The final qualifying session followed a similar pattern to the day before, with the Williams cars setting the pace and Schumacher pushing hard behind them. Mansell had one or two scares, but the new reactive suspension on his FW14B car served him well over the bumpy track. He was in pole position, followed by Patrese and the two Benetton drivers, Schumacher and Martin Brundle. The two McLaren's were fifth and sixth.

The warm-up confirmed Williams' dominance, though on the lap prior to the grid, Mansell experienced some problem with the steering and the team were frantically sorting out the problem while the car was on the grid. In the event, there was nothing to worry about, as Mansell used the new traction controlled system to its full effect as the light turned green.

The two Williams, with Mansell leading, led the rest of the pack into the first bend, prior to which a start-line accident had led to the almost immediate withdrawal of Ivan Capelli's Ferrari. Mansell was leading by more than a second after the first lap, though Patrese refused to let him get away.

For the first half of the race the two drivers swapped fast lap times over and over again, before a tyre problem on lap 26 forced Patrese to slow down. Senna, who was still in some pain from his earlier crash, managed to get a great start and was looking comfortable in third place. However, after 12 laps he pulled off the circuit with clutch problems.

With Mansell and Patrese in full control up front, the battle was on for the lower places. Michael Schumacher realised his potential with a fine drive in third place, while Gerhard Berger took fourth after a fine battle with Martin Brundle, who's race finished when his engine seized on lap 48.

It was another one-two for the Williams team. Ironically, both Mansell and Patrese felt that their cars, with their active suspensions, weren't that much assistance on the viciously uneven track. "Last year we were faster and the ride was better, so we'll have to look at this and see how we can improve," Mansell explained after his victory.

Williams had managed maximum points from the first two races of the season and, more importantly for Mansell, he had established an eight point lead at the top of the Championship table. The signs were looking ominous for the other teams, particularly McLaren, who were only too aware of the dominance shown by the increasingly confident British driver and the Williams team. ■

The Mexican Grand Prix

The Williams-Renault team arrived in Mexico as firm favourites. Nigel Mansell again taking pole from second placed Riccardo Patrese. In the race they didn't disappoint (right). Nigel took his second win ahead of Riccardo, the FW14B's active suspension handling Mexico's bumps better than any other.

CANON WILLIAMS TEAM
RENAULT
F1
CAMEL
Canon
CAMEL
CAMEL
Canon
Labatt's
Labatt's
Labatt's
RENAULT
elf
GOODYEAR
EAGLE

ARISTOS
ARISTOS
Canon

The Autodromo Hermanos Rodriguez:

5,000 ft above sea level: hot, bumpy and ultra fast.

Mansell leads the field in the dash to the first chicane.

1992

Marlboro
Marlboro
HONDA
COURTAULDS
COURTAULDS
Marlboro
HONDA
1
CAMEL
CAMEL
CAMEL
UNITED COLORS OF BENETTON
Ford
Ford
Ford
Mobil
20
SANYO
SANYO

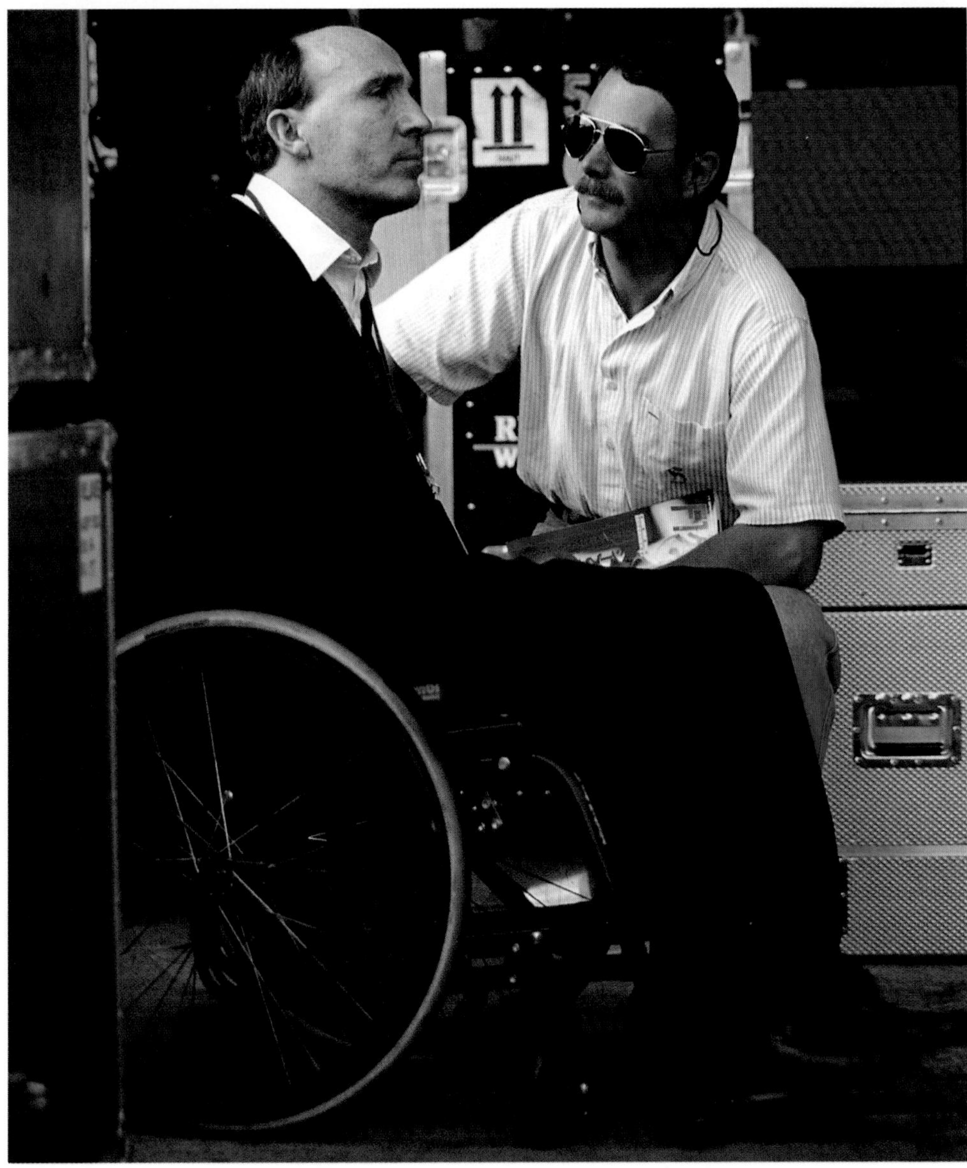

Mexican Grand Prix Results

22 March • 69 laps, 189.543 miles

Starting Positions

1	N Mansell	2	R Patrese
3	M Schumacher	4	M Brundle
5	G Berger	6	A Senna
7	JJ Lehto	8	M Gugelmin
9	P Martini	10	J Alesi

Finishing Positions and points

1	N Mansell	GB	Williams-Renault	10
2	R Patrese	Italy	Williams-Renault	6
3	M Schumacher	Germany	Benetton-Ford	4
4	G Berger	Germany	McLaren-Honda	3
5	A de Cesaris	Italy	Tyrell-Ilmor	2
6	M Hakkinen	Finland	Lotus-Ford	1

1992 Driver's Championship to date and points

1	N Mansell	20	2	R Patrese	8
3	M Schumacher	7	4	G Berger	5
5	A Senna	4	6	A de Cesaris	2
7	J Herbert	1	7	M Hakkinen	1

1992 Constructor's Championship to date and points

1	Williams-Renault	32
2	McLaren-Honda	9
3	Benetton-Ford	7
4	Tyrell-Ilmor	2
5	Lotus-Ford	2

Fastest Lap

Berger 1:17.711s (127.260 mph)

Ayrton Senna (top left) breaks down in Mexico. Afterwards he comlained bitterly to the McLaren team to try and hurry the completion of his new car. Martin Brundle (bottom left) in the Benetton, finds his car ever improving, and with it his confidence. (Top) The slow tranquility of South America with its natural beauty does nothing to slow Mansell's pace, unstoppable on Mexico's thirsty and dusty track. (Left) Nigel and team owner Frank Williams discuss tactics in the pits prior to the race. (Below) Perluigi Martini.

1992

Labatt's
elf
CAMEL
Labatt's
sparco
Labatt's
elf
CAMEL
Labatt's
sparco
Nigel Mansell
AUTO
Ma

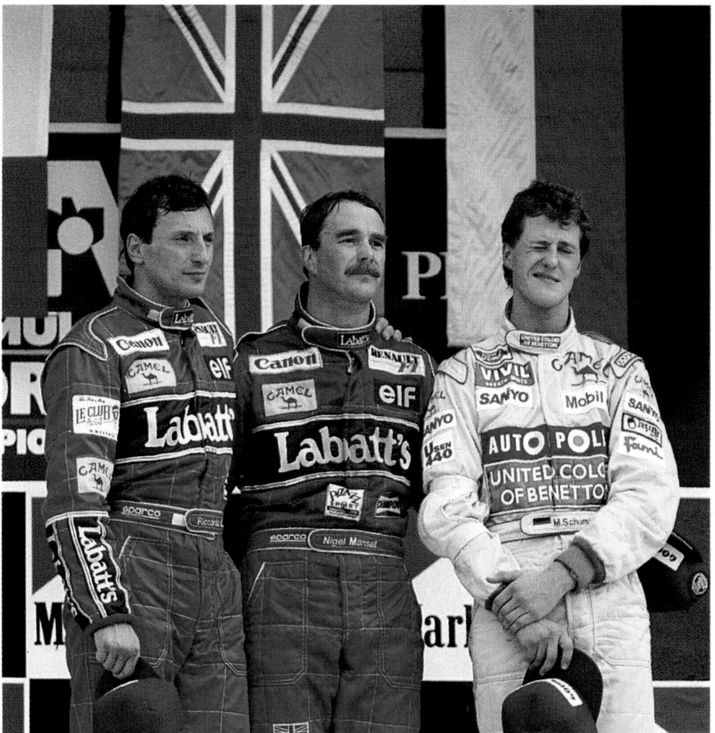

The Mexican Grand Prix

Mansell is joined by team-mate Patrese and 23 year old German 'Wunderkind' Michael Schumacher on the podium. The Williams duo are delighted at another 1st–2nd finish, while Schumacher is on the podium in only his eighth Formula One race.

1992

The Brazilian Grand Prix

Prior to the 1992 Brazilian Grand Prix, only a handful of drivers had achieved a hat-trick of wins on two different occasions. Jackie Stewart was the only Englishman in the exclusive club which also included Fangio, Lauda, Jones and Prost. Mansell had won three consecutive races once before, and was determined to repeat the feat at the twisting Interlagos circuit.

Judging by the events of the first two rounds of the Championship, it was going to take some exceptional circumstances to upset the superiority shown by Mansell and the Williams team. McLaren were ready to introduce their long-awaited MP4/7A's, with the fly-by-wire technology, which they hoped would be capable of upsetting the order.

But on the evidence of the first practice session this was not to be; Mansell and Patrese again eased their way round the track in the fastest times of the day, while Senna could only manage fifth.

The new McLaren's had failed their first test, and worse news was to come. In the first qualifying session Mansell put in one of the finest displays of driving in his twelve year career, recording a lap time which even his talented team-mate found difficult to get close to. What's more, his time of 1 min 15.703 seconds, at an average speed of 127.799 mph, broke Ayrton Senna's record pole time set the year before. It was another massive psychological boost for the Williams team, and another crushing blow for their opponents.

"It was a special lap," said Mansell. "When you go through the fast corners and then analyse it, you ask yourself if you could have gone quicker. I could not have gone quicker. That's when you know you've done a really hot lap. You know that given another 100 times, and another 100 sets of tyres, you could not have gone quicker."

During the Saturday practice sessions, the McLaren team went through their cars like they were going out of fashion, but at least Senna and Berger managed third and fourth place on the grid behind the Williams pair. Mansell had a scare when he was shunted by Senna late in the afternoon, and spun into a wall. He received a slight concussion, but was still full of confidence for the following day.

His confidence proved well founded. As the lights turned green, the Williams pair were again leading into the first corner, but this time it was Patrese who was out in front.

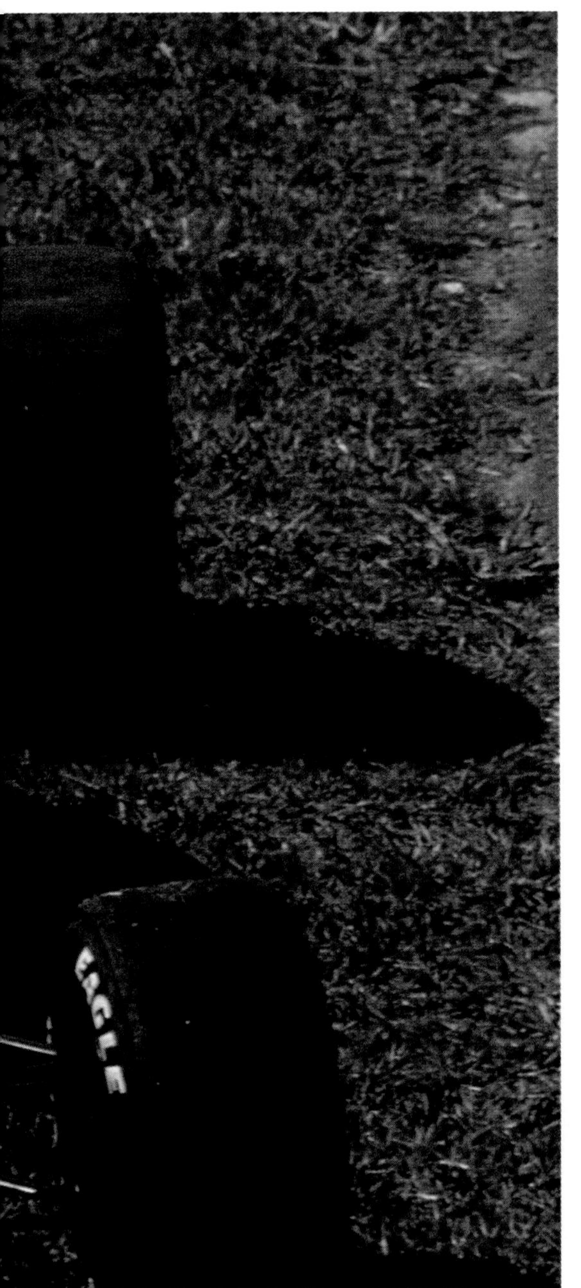

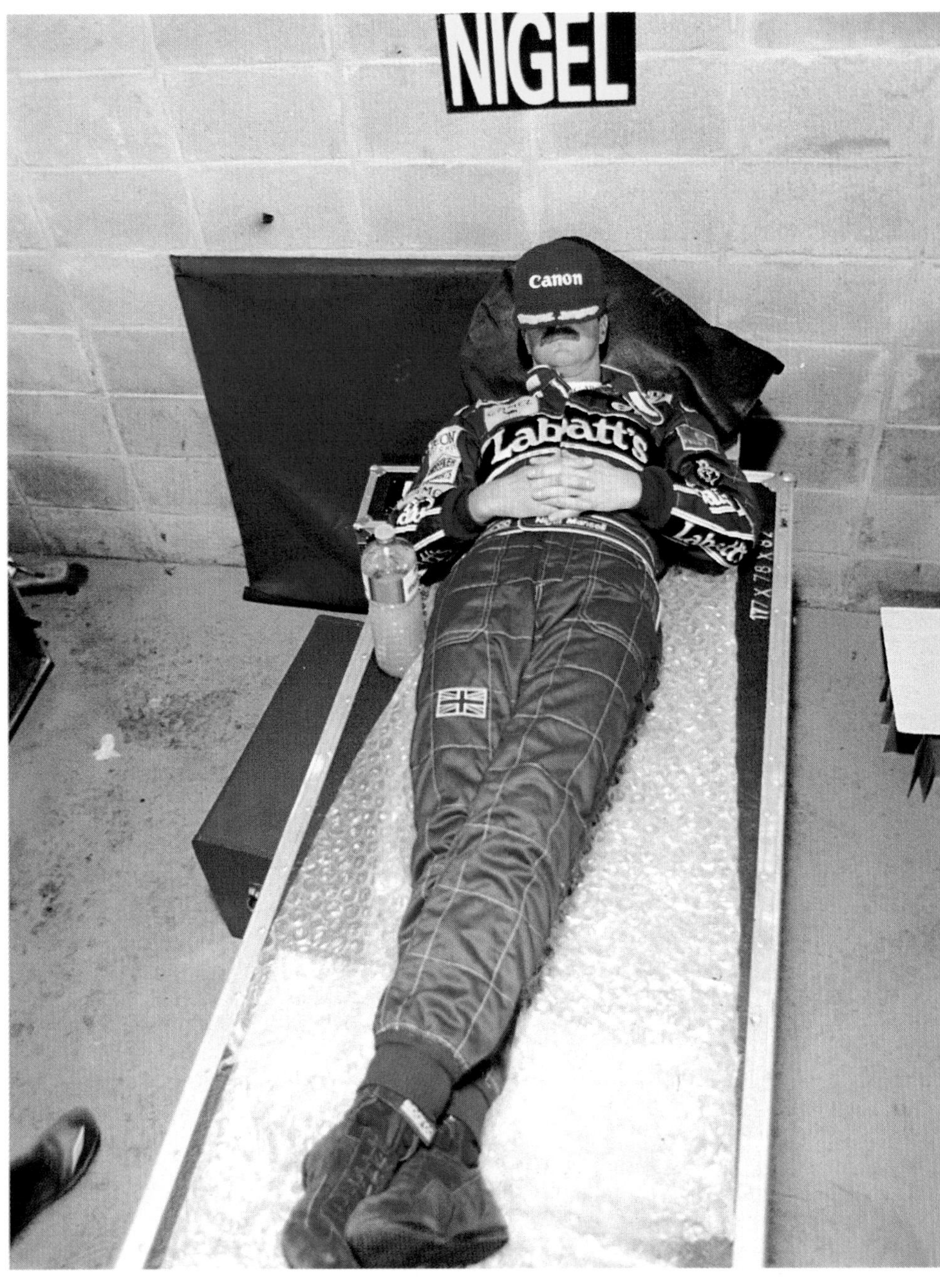

Mansell had got a poor start, sliding and wheel-spinning, and was thankful to still be in the race.

On lap 29, Mansell pitted for a tyre change. Patrese followed suit on lap 31. When the stops unwound, the Englishman found himself out in front, and once there he never looked back. He took the chequered flag 28 seconds ahead of Patrese, who completed his own hat-trick of second places ahead of the ever-improving Michael Schumacher.

Meanwhile, the McLarens had a disastrous day. Despite bringing six cars and a 100-strong team, neither of their drivers managed to finish. Gerhard Berger lasted just four laps, while an electrical fault forced Senna to retire on lap 16. The World Champions had obviously introduced their 'fly-by-wire' too early.

It was another clean sweep for Mansell and Williams, and their lead was starting to look unassailable. But after the race Mansell refused to discuss his prospects of winning the Championship, pointing out the dangers of complacency. He remembered only too well how McLaren won the first four races of the 1991 season, while Williams had failed to pick up a point.

"I remember last year – and I know what McLaren are capable of doing," he remarked after the race. He was sensibly taking each race one at a time. ■

The Brazilian Grand Prix

(Top left) Nigel Mansell gets rattled and crashes in practice after tangling with arch rival Senna's McLaren. More relaxed before the race (above) he sweeps to his third victory on Sunday (right).

The Winning Team

'Red Five' comes alive in Brazil.

Labatt's
Canon
RENAULT
RENAULT
elf
5
MAGNETI
MARELLI
GOODYEAR
Canon
Canon

1992

Brazilian Grand Prix Results

5 April • 71 laps, 190.807 miles

Starting Positions

1	N Mansell	2	R Patrese
3	A Senna	4	G Berger
5	M Schumacher	6	J Alesi
7	M Brundle	8	P Martini
9	K Wendlinger	10	T Boutsen

Finishing Positions and points

1	N Mansell	GB	Williams-Renault	10
2	R Patrese	Italy	Williams-Renault	6
3	M Schumacher	Germany	Benetton-Ford	4
4	J Alesi	France	Ferrari	3
5	I Capelli	Italy	Ferrari	2
6	M Albereto	Italy	Footwork-Mugen	1

1992 Driver's Championship to date and points

1	N Mansell	30	2	R Patrese	18
3	M Schumacher	11	4	G Berger	5
5	A Senna	4	6	J Alesi	3
7	A de Cesaris	2	7	I Capelli	2
9	J Herbert	1	9	M Hakkinen	1
9	M Alboreto	1			

1992 Constructor's Championship to date and points

1	Williams-Renault	48
2	Benetton-Ford	11
3	McLaren-Honda	9
4	Ferrari	5
5	Tyrell-Ilmor	2
	Lotus-Ford	2
7	Footwork-Mugen	1

Fastest Lap

Patrese 1:19.490s (121.710 mph)

The Brazilian Grand Prix

(Top left) The new McLaren MP4/7 does not help Senna who retired on lap 17, whilst Mansell (left) pulls away to win. The car's new traction control helping him in the corners (right). Michael Schumacher (below) impresses again in the Benetton.

50
100
Shell
+26·8
NIGEL
WINS
Canon
RENAULT
Labatt's
elf
Canon
CAMEL
Mansell
RENAULT

Brazilian Grand Prix – Sao Paulo.

A justifiably delighted Mansell crosses the line having lapped the whole field with the exception of Patrese.

1992

The Spanish Grand Prix

The question on everybody's mind during the lead-up to the Spanish Grand Prix, was who, or what, was going to stop the Williams team dominating the rest of the season? The last time a non Williams-Renault car led a Grand Prix was in Adelaide in 1991, and it was becoming increasingly obvious that the Williams cars were in a class of their own.

The first practice session at the Circuit de Catalunya told the same old story, with Mansell and Patrese again heading the lap times. But in the afternoon Patrese experienced some difficulties with this car, and this allowed Schumacher, who spun and hit a wall later in the session, and Senna to record quicker times. And then it started to rain.

Come Saturday morning, the conditions were appalling. There was so much water about that few of the teams wanted to risk damaging their cars and settled for the overnight grid positions. A few drivers braved the wet track, particularly Jean Alesi in his Ferrari, but it made no difference to the grid.

With little let-up in the rain on the day of the race, the other teams were hoping the conditions would work in their favour. The Patrick Head designed FW/14's had asserted their superiority time and time again in dry conditions, but would they prove quite as suited to a rain-soaked circuit?

The answer was an emphatic yes. The Williams drivers took up their usual positions at the front, after the anti-skid devices on their cars had given both of them excellent starts. Jean Alesi got an even better start, and from eighth place on the grid he managed to work his way into second by the time they reached the first corner.

By lap five, Mansell was 3.7 seconds ahead of Patrese, who in turn, was a further 10 seconds clear of the rest of the field. After 15 laps they were 20 seconds ahead of the third placed Schumacher. Senna was fourth in his MP4/7 which appeared to be running far better than when McLaren first introduced it in the Brazilian Grand Prix.

But things were soon to change. On the 20th lap Patrese lost some downforce while coming up behind a back-marker, the car spun away from him and hit a wall. This left Mansell with a 22 second lead over Schumacher who was comfortably holding off the two McLarens.

In the second half of the race, the rain got gradually worse, and it was at this stage that Schumacher started to threaten Mansell's lead. On the 50th lap the gap was down to 4.5 seconds, and many a spectator started to think the unthinkable. But all of a sudden Mansell stepped up a gear, almost as if he had been driving with something in reverse. By lap 55 he had re-asserted himself and the lead was back to 16 seconds, and he proceeded to ease his way through the last ten laps.

Michael Schumacher, who had earlier signalled for the race to be called off, continued his remarkable season by taking second place. He finished 2.5 seconds ahead of Jean Alesi, who as always drove an all-or-nothing race. Twice he spun off and twice he raced back on to the track, getting more out of his Ferrari than even he thought possible.

But once again the day belonged to Nigel Mansell, who drove a faultless race as he lead from start to finish. "There is never a single reason why one wins," he explained later in the day. "It is like a chain. If one of the links is weak, then the chain will break. But the foundations of this team are deep and sound."

It was the 25th win of Mansell's career, bringing him alongside Jim Clark and Niki Lauda in the record books, and by claiming his fourth consecutive victory, he equalled Ayrton Senna's record for the best ever start to a Formula One season. The chain was certainly holding strong. ■

The Spanish Grand Prix

(Above) The cars pull away from a damp grid with Mansell at the fore. (Right) Again, Red Five would not be beaten all day.

AULT
elf

Mansell keeps it together as he leads the field throughout the first lap in atrocious conditions.

In the background, Chiesa spins on to the grass.

Canon
Marlboro
Canon

The Spanish Grand Prix

Nigel tip-toes around the soaking Barcelona track (above, right and mid-right). (Below) His car pitching and sliding this way and that in the Sunday rains following Friday's dry qualifying rounds. (Far right) Nigel's fourth champagne fight of the year.

Spanish Grand Prix Results

3 May • 65 laps, 191.681 miles

Starting Positions

1	N Mansell	2	M Schumacher
3	A Senna	4	R Patrese
5	J Capelli	6	M Brundle
7	G Berger	8	J Alesi
9	K Wendlinger	10	E Comas

Finishing Positions and points

1	N Mansell	GB	Williams-Renault	10
2	M Schumacher	Germany	Benetton-Ford	6
3	J Alesi	France	Ferrari	4
4	G Berger	Austria	McLaren-Honda	3
5	M Albereto	Italy	Footwork-Mugen	2
6	P Martini	Italy	Dallara-Ferrari	1

1992 Driver's Championship to date and points

1	N Mansell	40	2	R Patrese	18
3	M Schumacher	17	4	G Berger	8
5	J Alesi	7	6	A Senna	4
7	M Alboreto	3	8	A de Cesaris	2
8	I Capelli	2	10	J Herbert	1
10	M Hakkinen	1	10	P Martini	1

1992 Constructor's Championship to date and points

1	Williams-Renault	58
2	Benetton-Ford	17
3	McLaren-Honda	12
4	Ferrari	9
5	Footwork-Mugen	3
6	Tyrell-Ilmor	2
	Lotus-Ford	2
8	Dallara-Ferrari	1

Fastest Lap

Mansell 1:42.503s (103/594 mph)

Canon
Labatt's
canon
GOODYEAR
RENAULT
canon

CAMEL
elf
elf
5
Bull

1992

The San Marino Grand Prix

During his Formula One career, Nigel Mansell has earned praise and respect from all quarters for his driving. On occasions his temperament has been questioned, but few have doubted his skill, determination and courage. It was these qualities that made him such a favourite with the fanatical Ferrari followers – the tifosi – and even though his allegiance was now with another team, he was still a very popular figure in Italy.

As the temperatures reached the high 80's and with the tifosi encamped on the hillside overlooking the Autodromo Enzo e Dino Ferrari, Il Leone was in a confident mood. There was little doubt that he would again give his all in an effort to go further ahead in the Drivers' Championship.

The Friday session confirmed this. In the morning there was little to separate Mansell and Ayrton Senna's McLaren. But by the end of the afternoon session the gap was firmly established as the Englishman showed his class in recording a time more than a second faster than the second-placed Patrese.

"That was a special lap," Mansell said after the session. "I am very happy with it. It was a second quicker than any other lap I did. It was almost perfect. I was ready for it, the tyres came in at just the right time and, most importantly of all, I had no traffic."

By the end of the qualifying, the Williams pair had once again taken the first two positions on the grid, followed by the McLaren's of Ayrton Senna and Gerhard Berger. Michael Schumacher was in fifth.

As the cars lined up for the start of the race, Mansell, again fastest in the warm-up, was having problems with this clutch, and as the lights turned green he had trouble getting away. But fortunately for him Karl Wendlinger had stalled his March, and the start was aborted.

This gave the Williams team time to fix the clutch, and on the re-start Mansell made the most of his luck and built up a lead of almost two seconds after the first lap. By the end of lap five he was 3.6 seconds ahead of Patrese who in turn had a 12 second lead over Senna in third place.

On lap 23 Mansell went into the pits for a tyre change and on his return to the track he was surprised to find himself still out in front. Patrese, who had changed his tyres a few laps earlier threatened briefly, but as Mansell pushed again his Italian team-mate was left

behind. Neither driver was troubled for the rest of the afternoon.

The real race was for third place, where the two McLarens were pressuring Jean Alesi in his Ferrari. Alesi had been doing a fine job of keeping them at bay, but on lap 40 Senna squeezed past, and as Berger attempted the same, the Ferrari and McLaren touched wheels. They both spun out leaving the exhausted Senna to take third, with Martin Brundle in fourth.

Nigel Mansell and the Williams team had done it again. Their victory at Imola was their fifth consecutive season-opening win, breaking the record set by Ayrton Senna in 1991, and their fourth 'one-two' success in five races. The Williams-Renault cars showed once more that in terms of sheer speed and power, none of their rivals could touch them, and with Nigel Mansell at the wheel, the partnership was proving invincible. ■

The Spanish Grand Prix

(Above) Nigel Mansell watches his rival's times on the monitor before going fastesr in each of the sessions (top left) to claim his fifth consecutive pole position of the season.

The San Marino Grand Prix
(Top) Nigel Mansell rushes into the record books with his fifth win out of five races, again leading from the start (above right) to finish in front of team-mate Riccardo Patrese (far right). The Italian crowd had little to cheer about, when Jean Alesi (right) and Ivan Capelli's Ferraris both failed to finish.

ICEBE
Marlboro
Marlboro
elf
5
elf
6
CAMEL
CAMEL
elf
RENAULT
Labatt's
6
Labatt's
Labatt's
canon
Bull

Red Five sets an all time record of five consecutive wins at the start of the season when he leads the San Marino Grand Prix from start to finish.

San Marino Grand Prix Results

17 May • 60 laps, 187.920 miles

Starting Positions

1	N Mansell	2	R Patrese
3	A Senna	4	G Berger
5	M Schumacher	6	M Brundle
7	J Alesi	8	J Capelli
9	M Alboreto	10	T Boutsen

Finishing Positions and points

1	N Mansell	GB	Williams-Renault	10
2	R Patrese	Italy	Williams-Renault	6
3	A Senna	Brazil	McLaren-Honda	4
4	M Brundle	GB	Benetton-Ford	3
5	M Alboreto	Italy	Footwork-Mugen	2
6	P Martini	Italy	Dallara-Ferrari	1

1992 Driver's Championship to date and points

1	N Mansell	50	2	R Patrese	24
3	M Schumacher	17	4	A Senna	8
4	G Berger	8	6	J Alesi	7
7	M Alboreto	5	8	M Brundle	3
9	A de Cesaris	2	9	I Capelli	2
9	P Martini	2	12	J Herbert	1
12	M Hakkinen	1			

1992 Constructor's Championship to date and points

1	Williams-Renault	74
2	Benetton-Ford	20
3	McLaren-Honda	16
4	Ferrari	9
5	Footwork-Mugen	5
6	Tyrell-Ilmor	2
	Lotus-Ford	2
	Dallara-Ferrari	2

Fastest Lap

Patrese 1:26.100s (130.943 mph)

The San Marino Grand Prix
(Above left) Nigel holds aloft his fifth winner's trophy of '92, whilst celebrating another 1st–2nd, with Patrese (above). (Below left) The leaders climb the hill to Piratella on the fabulous Imola circuit. Michele Alboreto (below), the only other driver to have finished every race is 5th. (Below right) Britain's Martin Brundle showing well in fourth.

1992

The Monaco Grand Prix

The next stop for the Formula One roadshow was the glitzy principality of Monaco, where the tight track twists its way through the streets of high-rise apartment blocks, and along the yacht-lined stretches of the Mediterranean.

Held every year on Ascension Day weekend, the Monaco Grand Prix is regarded as one of the highlights of the Formula One season. With its sumptuous harbour and glamourous nightlife, Monaco provides the ideal setting for the teams to show off what they can do, in an effort to attract the cheque books of major sponsors. Every one is keen to impress and consequently a little on edge.

However, none of this looked likely to upset the dominant Williams team, as Mansell recorded the fastest lap during Thursday's qualifying sessions. Patrese took third on a day when there were spins and slides everywhere, with most drivers complaining about too much traffic on a tight circuit.

After playing golf on the traditional Friday off, Nigel Mansell returned to the track on Saturday and, after swapping fastest times with team-mate Patrese, took pole position once again. Patrese was second, followed by Senna and Alesi.

It proved to be the most exciting qualifying session of the year so far, as each driver did their best to improve on their

Thursday times. Overtaking is extremely difficult on the Monaco circuit and consequently it is very important to start from a good position.

Surprisingly Mansell was only fifth fastest in the warm-up – he was unable to get a clear lap- but this made little difference to the start, and he took his customary place up front. Senna used all his experience to squeeze past Patrese and was second as they approached the first right hand corner and the hill towards Casino Square.

Senna attempted to tuck in behind Mansell, but by the end of the 4th lap the Englishman had a 5 second lead. After 18 laps it was 14 seconds, and on lap 60 it increased even more after Senna was blocked by Michele Alboreto who had taken a spin. It all looked set for the Williams driver to record his first victory at Monaco.

But on lap 71 Mansell took a pit stop, complaining of a problem with one of his tyres, and this gave Senna the break he had been looking for. After a lengthy tyre change the Williams driver returned to the track only to see Senna marginally in front. A non-Williams car was actually leading a 1992 Grand Prix!

It didn't take Mansell long to make-up the 5 second deficit, and with three laps to go he was right on Senna's tail. But the Brazilian kept his line well as Mansell tried everything he could to pass him. However, it was all to no avail as Senna took the chequered flag two tenths of a second ahead of Mansell, depriving him of what looked likely to be his first Monaco victory.

Mansell was gracious in defeat and said after the race, "Ayrton was perfectly entitled to do what he did, to defend his position. It was regrettable that the tyre change took a few seconds longer than usual, because otherwise I could perhaps have rejoined the race without losing the lead."

It was Mansell's first defeat of the season. Despite leading for seven-eighths of the race, he was again the unfortunate victim of some cruel luck. However, even though he failed to record his first win in Monaco, or match Alberto Ascari's 40 year-old record of six successive Grand Prix wins, he did manage to collect 6 points in second place and extend his championship lead to 28 points. His season was still well on course. ■

(Far left) A visibly happy Nigel Mansell went to Monaco with a 26 point lead, refusing to talk about his Championship prospects, preferring to spend time with his wife, Roseanne and children, Chloe, Greg and Leo (above).

AMPION
CHAMPION
Marlboro
Marlboro
CAMEL
Canon
elf
Canon
HITACHI

As the field screams down into San Devot for the first time, Nigel is clear in the lead. Behind in the midfield, de Cesaris starts to lock up.

The Monaco Grand Prix *(Above and below) Ayrton Senna fought his car ahead of Patrese, but could not come close to Mansell as he pulled away (right). Johnny Herbert (below right) put in another spirited drive for the resurgent Lotus team. Both Benettons scored points (bottom mid- and far-right), Brundle in 5th and Schumacher in 4th after a titanic battle with Patrese.*

Labatt's
Canon
RENAULT
elf
5
MAGNETI MARELLI

EBERG
Marlboro
ICEBERG
NICE

Gatorade
HITACHI
FOSTERS
Marlboro

1992

The Monaco Grand Prix
(Left and right) Mansell flies around Monaco with 6 laps remaining to catch Senna, breaking the track record lap after lap until finally (far left) he is on the McLaren's gearbox. Unable to find a way past on the tight circuit, he finishes 0.15 seconds behind Ayrton.

Labatt's
RENAULT
elf
5
MAGNETI MARELLI

The Monaco Grand Prix

(Above) Nigel collapses with exhaustion after the race and is helped to his feet by Ayrton Senna. (Below and right) The strains and exertions of driving at and above the limits are clearly visible in Nigel's face.

Monaco Grand Prix Results

31 May • 78 laps, 161.298 miles

Starting Positions

1	N Mansell	2	R Patrese
3	A Senna	4	J Alesi
5	G Berger	6	M Schumacher
7	M Brundle	8	I Capelli
9	J Herbert	10	A de Cesaris

Finishing Positions and points

1	A Senna	Brazil	McLaren-Honda	10
2	N Mansell	GB	Williams-Renault	6
3	R Patrese	Italy	Williams-Renault	4
4	M Schumacher	Germany	Benetton-Ford	3
5	M Brundle	GB	Benetton-Ford	2
6	B Gachot	Belgium	Venturi-Lamborghini	1

1992 Driver's Championship to date and points

1	N Mansell	56	2	R Patrese	28
3	M Schumacher	20	4	A Senna	18
5	G Berger	8	6	J Alesi	7
7	M Brundle	5	7	M Alboreto	5
9	A de Cesaris	2	9	I Capelli	2
9	P Martini	2			

1992 Constructor's Championship to date and points

1	Williams-Renault	84
2	McLaren-Honda	26
3	Benetton-Ford	25
4	Ferrari	9
5	Footwork-Mugen	5
6	Tyrell-Ilmor	2
	Lotus-Ford	2
	Dallara-Ferrari	2
	Venturi-Lamborghini	1

Fastest Lap

Mansell 1:21.598 (91.234 mph)

CAMEL

1992

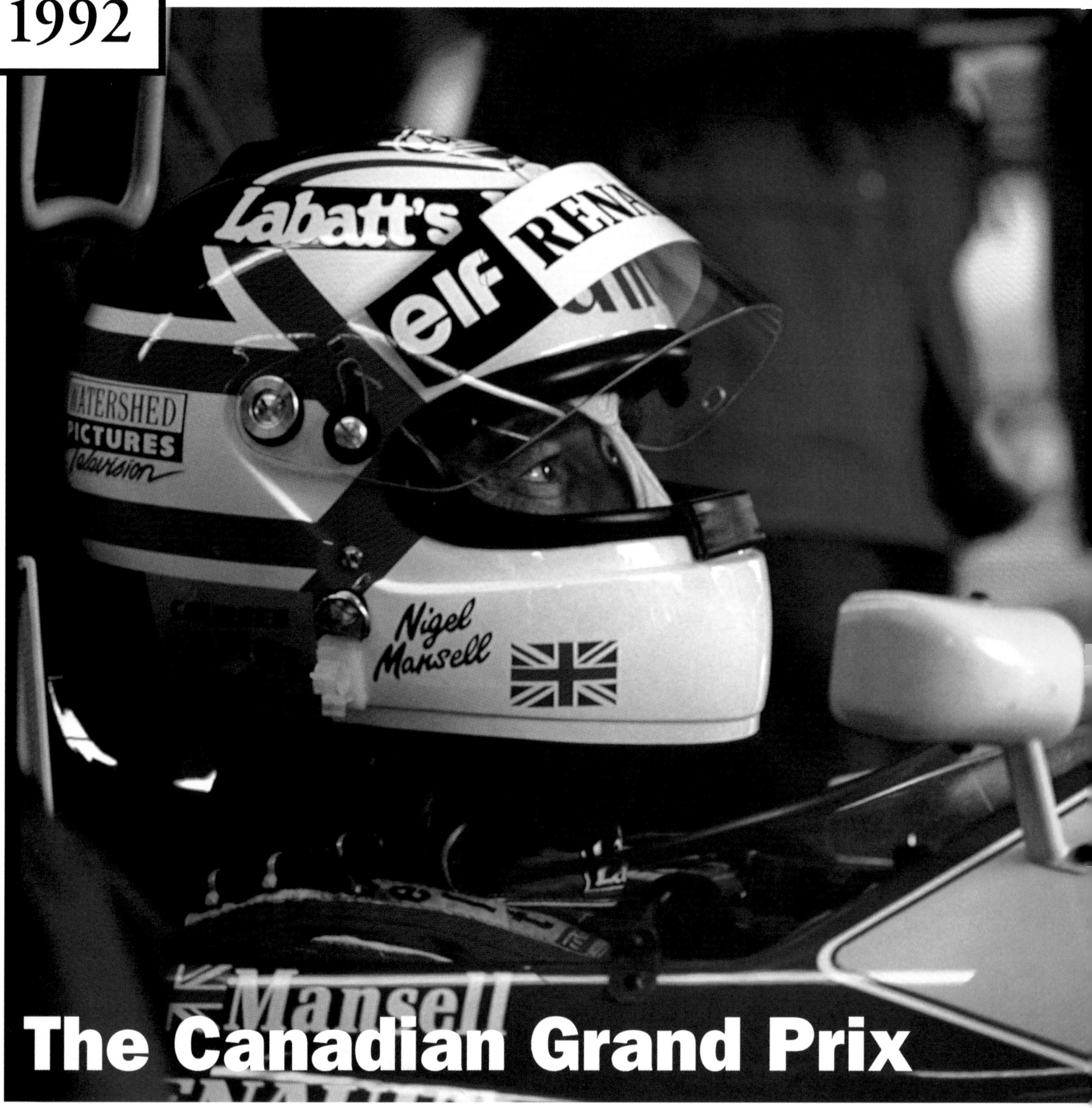

The Canadian Grand Prix

After the events in Monaco, the McLaren team were understandably relieved to be back to their winning ways, and were now more confident of being able to supply their drivers with cars that could actually challenge the Williams domination. The MP4/7A had gradually improved since it was first introduced in Brazil, but most observers believed it still had some way to go before it could match the Patrick Head designed cars.

The first practice on the Gilles Villeneuve circuit was evidence that the McLarens had indeed moved forward. On a day when the wind, rain and uneven nature of the track caused difficulties for most of the drivers, Ayrton Senna was fastest in both the free session and the qualifying session, while Mansell could only manage fourth. It was proof of the advances made by Honda in engine power, and McLaren in chassis performance.

As Mansell said after the first day, "I think this proves what I have been saying for some time. Namely, that the Honda engine is ahead on power... I know people have been making it seem easy for me, but it isn't and this proves it."

Mansell managed to improve his lap times during the Saturday sessions, but it was

The Canadian Grand Prix

(Left) The pressure of a World Championship for the taking begins to show in Nigel. For the first time in 1992 he is not on pole but qualifying (below) leaves him in third place.

only quick enough to take him into third place behind Senna, who recorded his first pole position of the season. Patrese was second on the grid and Berger fourth, making the contest much the same as always – Williams versus McLaren.

At the start Mansell got away well, and though he managed to overtake his team-mate before the first bend, Senna was still in front at the end of the first lap. Overtaking is not easy in Montreal, and the Brazilian sensibly decided that a controlled drive in the early stages of the race would be enough to keep him ahead of Mansell, Patrese and Berger.

On lap 15 the order of the race changed dramatically. Mansell, keen to get out front and build up a lead, attempted to overtake Senna as they approached the final corner, a tight left-right twist before the pit straight. Senna resisted the Englishman's efforts to pass him, and Mansell was unable to control his car as it careered off across a sand trap, before coming to rest on the track in front of the other cars. Mansell's car was without its nose cone, and he was out of the race.

As is usual in Formula One, both drivers defended their actions. Mansell accused Senna of shunting him off the track, while the McLaren driver claimed that Mansell failed to break in time for the bend and consequently had to try and ride the kerb and the sand trap.

Irrespective of who was at fault, the reality of the situation was that Mansell was out of a Grand Prix for the first time in the season. What's more, in the ensuing confusion Berger managed to squeeze past Patrese, and suddenly the two McLaren's were out in front. Patrese was third, with the Benettons in fourth and fifth.

This was how the order stayed until lap 38, when ironically Senna's engine cut-out, and he had to retire. This gave his team-mate Gerhard Berger the lead, with Patrese following in second until a gear problem forced him out on the 44th lap. Berger went on to complete his first victory of the season, with Michael Schumacher continuing his meteoric rise in second and Jean Alesi taking third.

McLaren had recorded their second successive victory, while Mansell's championship hopes had suffered another set-back. He may not have won in Monaco, but at least he picked up six points for second place. In Montreal he failed to add any points to his championship total. The one consolation for Mansell was that the result made little difference to the standing in the Drivers' Championship – he was still 28 points clear. ■

canon
canon
GOODYEAR

Nigel Mansell's is the world's most expensive car.

Extras include traction control, active suspension, semi-automatic gearbox... but no choice of colour-scheme.

1992

Canadian Grand Prix Results

14 June • 69 laps, 189.934 miles

Starting Positions

1	A Senna	2	R Patrese
3	N Mansell	4	G Berger
5	M Schumacher	6	J Herbert
7	M Brundle	8	J Alesi
9	I Capelli	10	M Hakkinen

Finishing Positions and points

1	G Berger	Austria	McLaren-Honda	10
2	M Schumacher	Germany	Benetton-Ford	6
3	J Alesi	France	Ferrari	4
4	K Wendlinger	Austria	March-Ilmor	3
5	A de Cesaris	Italy	Tyrell-Ilmor	2
6	E Comas	France	Ligier-Renault	1

1992 Driver's Championship to date and points

1	N Mansell	56	2	R Patrese	28
3	M Schumacher	26	4	A Senna	18
4	G Berger	18	6	J Alesi	11
7	M Brundle	5	7	M Alboreto	5
9	A de Cesaris	4	10	K Wendlinger	3
11	I Capelli	2	11	P Martini	2
13	J Herbert	1	13	M Hakkinen	1
13	B Gachot	1	13	E Comas	1

1992 Constructor's Championship to date and points

1	Williams-Renault	56
2	McLaren-Honda	36
3	Benetton-Ford	31
4	Ferrari	13
5	Footwork-Mugen	5
6	Tyrell-Ilmor	4

Fastest Lap

Mansell 1:22.325 (120.372 mph)

The Canadian Grand Prix

(Far left) Johnny Herbert continues to impress in the new Lotus 107. (Left) Gerhard Berger won his second race for McLaren after Senna (right) and Mansell (below) both retire. (Above) The stunning Michael Schumacher is second for Benetton.

Labatt's
CAMEL
GOODYEAR
RENAULT
elf
canon
Labatt's

Labat
Bull

1992

The French Grand Prix

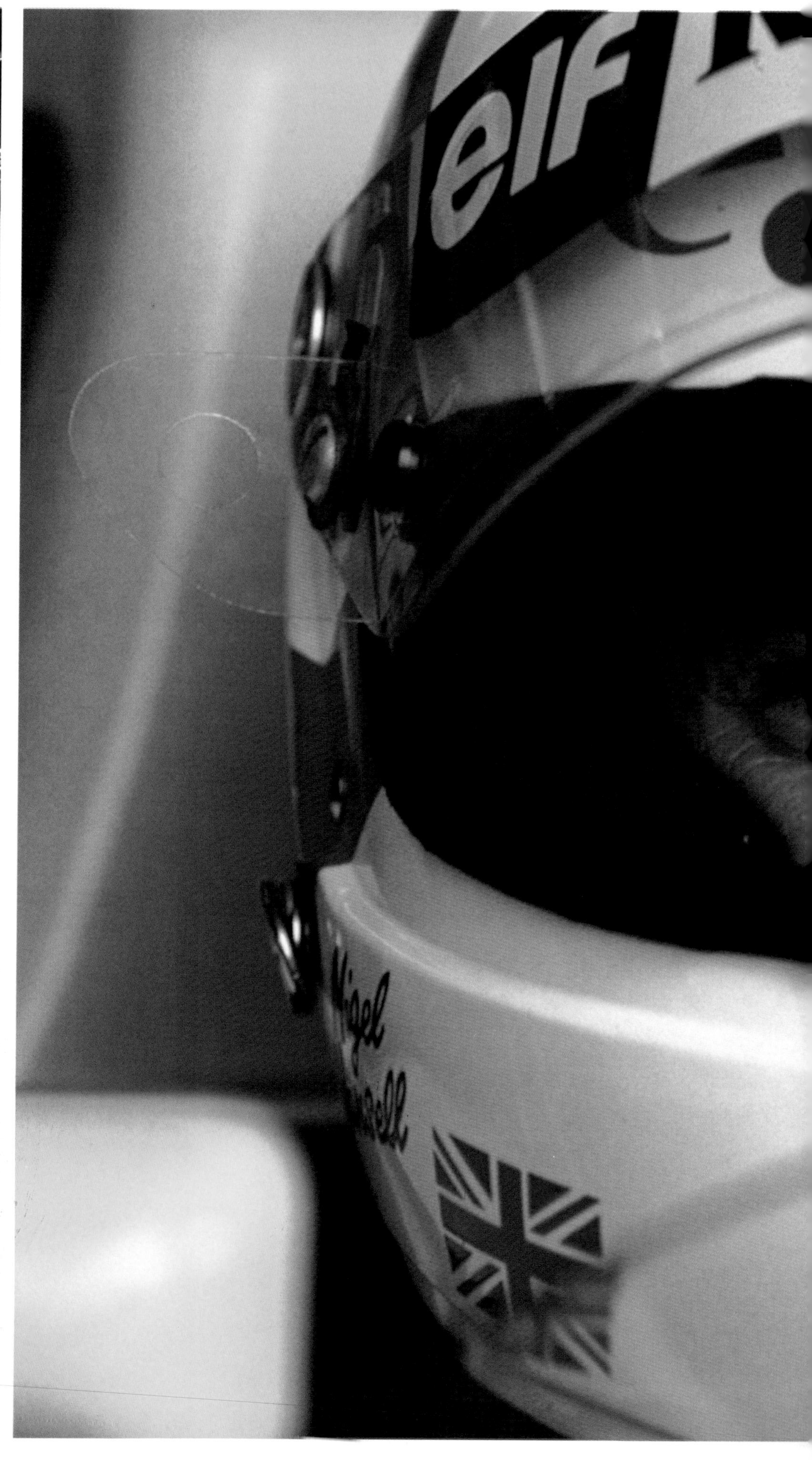

In 1991 Ayrton Senna and the McLaren team looked set to run away with the Formula One Championship, and it wasn't until the season was nearly half way through that Williams began to offer them any serious competition. The first half of the 1992 season had followed a similar pattern, but this time it was McLaren chasing Williams.

This fact was clear in the minds of both teams, and after the turn of events in Monaco and Montreal, Williams were all too aware of the dangers of complacency, while the McLaren team aren't the types to give up the battle while they are still in with a fighting chance.

As McLaren's team owner Ron Dennis pointed out prior to the French Grand Prix, "In a normal year, I would just about admit that the Championship is as good as over for us. But at the moment there are some emotional inconsistencies in other teams, and that may play in our favour." Dennis has never been one for throwing in the towel.

But first all the teams had to overcome the hurdle set by drivers of another kind – France was in the throws of an industrial dispute involving their lorry drivers. They had blockaded most of the country's main

highways and it was only with a good deal of forward planning and quick thinking that the Formula One roadshow arrived on time at the Magny-Cours race track.

After the first day of practice, Mansell was back in command, with a lap time half a second ahead of Patrese, who in turn was 1.3 seconds faster than Senna in third. On the second day, the times got quicker and quicker but there was little change to the grid order. The two Williams cars were followed by Senna and Berger, with Schumacher and Alesi sharing the third row.

Conditions were looking ominous on race day. However, it remained dry before the warm-up and as the lights turned green all 26 cars got away cleanly. Patrese got the best start and immediately took the lead. Meanwhile Ayrton Senna's race lasted less than a lap after he was hit from behind by Schumacher's Benetton, and Berger was forced to retire with a broken engine.

On lap 19, with Patrese still leading from Mansell, the heavens opened and a red flag went up to signal a halt to the race, allowing the teams time to change their tyres. Twenty minutes later the race re-started with the promise of an interesting battle between the two Williams men.

But it was not to be. Patrese was obviously under orders from the team, and after one more lap in front he moved over and waved his team-mate through. Mansell took the chance with both hands and went on to win by 46 seconds. Patrese was comfortable in second, while Mansell's fellow Englishman, Martin Brundle, had the best result of his career after a courageous and polished piece of driving.

It was the 26th win of Mansell's career, and with it he equalled Jackie Stewart's British record of Grand Prix wins, the third best ever behind Alain Prost and arch-rival Ayrton Senna. More importantly, the Williams team was back to its best after the recent set-backs. During the after-race press conference, Mansell still refused to talk about his World Championship chances, but with six wins out of eight races it didn't take an expert to realise that he was now comfortably back on course for that first elusive title. ■

The French Grand Prix

(Top left) Back in Europe and the Williams team were back on top again.
(Left) Nigel was fastest in every qualifying session, warm-up and in the race itself. But victory didn't come easy for him in the race – it appeared that there were team orders as Patrese allowed Mansell to pass him.

Marlboro
Marlboro

rlboro
Marlboro
Canon
Canon
6

Canon
Canon
Canon
Labatt's
Canon
RENAULT
elf
CAMEL
CAMEL
RACING SERVICE
Labatt's
Labatt's
RENAULT
elf
5
MAGNETI MARELLI
GOODYEAR
Canon

The French Grand Prix
(Left) Nigel Mansell set the pace all weekend at Magny-Cours, France. (Above) Mansell finally passes Riccardo Patrese after the restart. (Below) Senna used all the power his Honda could muster, but still found himself third on the grid. (Bottom) Race day would be worse still for Senna, who was shunted off on the first lap.

French Grand Prix Results

5 July • 69 laps, 183.126 miles

Starting Positions

1	N Mansell	2	R Patrese
3	A Senna	4	G Berger
5	M Schumacher	6	J Alesi
7	M Brundle	8	I Capelli
9	T Boutsen	10	E Comas

Finishing Positions and points

1	N Mansell	GB	Williams-Renault	10
2	R Patrese	Italy	Williams-Renault	6
3	M Brundle	GB	Benetton-Ford	4
4	M Hakkinen	Finland	Lotus-Ford	3
5	E Comas	France	Ligier-Renault	2
6	J Herbert	GB	Lotus-Ford	1

1992 Driver's Championship to date and points

1	N Mansell	66	2	R Patrese	34
3	M Schumacher	26	4	A Senna	18
4	G Berger	18	6	J Alesi	11
7	M Brundle	5	8	M Alboreto	5
9	M Hakkinen	4	9	A de Cesaris	4

1992 Constructor's Championship to date and points

1	Williams-Renault	100
2	McLaren-Honda	36
3	Benetton-Ford	35
4	Ferrari	13
5	Lotus-Ford	6
6	Footwork-Mugen	5

Fastest Lap

Mansell 1:17.070 (123.355 mph)

The French Grand Prix

(Top) Mansell begins to pull away from Patrese while behind follows Britain's Johnny Herbert (left) who finishes 6th in the points and Martin Brundle (bottom left) on the podium in third place (right). (Below) Jean Alesi flew in the wet on slick tyres before his engine blew up.

RHÔNE-POULENC
GOODYEAR
Canon
Labatt's
elf
Mobil
VIVIL
M.Brundle

1992

The British Grand Prix

In 1986 Mansell was voted Sports Personality of the Year by the British public. As we know, he had been desperately unlucky in his bid to win the Drivers World Championship that year, but the truth of the matter was that he had not won. And yet he was still the most popular sportsman in Britain! He had become a hero in the mould of the classic British loser – a good effort, but not quite good enough.

Mansell did not crave this kind of attention. He felt awkward with this title because he still had to realise his full potential and reach his goal, and this image of a gallant loser did not lie comfortably with his competitive and single-minded nature. He wanted recognition for success, rather than for his valiant efforts.

Over the years Mansell has made the converted RAF airfield at Silverstone his home track, as the fast and demanding circuit suits his all-or-nothing style. In 1991, he won there in front of his adoring fans – fans who have supported him through the highs and lows of his career without ever doubting his ability as a driver. He could think of no better way of repaying them than by producing another winning display in what was looking more and more likely to be his year. Mansell-mania had hit Britain and he was determined to give them something to cheer.

An estimated 40,000 people turned up to watch the first day of practice and Mansell returned the compliment by putting in one of the finest qualifying displays of his career. In the first session he broke his own testing record of 1m20.56s on three different occasions, he was 1.1 seconds quicker than fellow driver Patrese, and 2.48 seconds quicker than Senna in third.

More was to come. In the afternoon Mansell broke his best time again, and then again, until he finally put in a lap which left most on-lookers agape. The clock stopped at a remarkable 1m18.965s, a time that even Mansell found astonishing. "That was a spectacular session and a perfect lap," he said afterwards. "I was so quick. I can't imagine going any quicker than that."

"Silverstone is a track which demands total commitment and that's what I always have when I'm in a racing car. Believe me, my quickest lap was quite something. I could hardly believe the speed at which I was going through Copse. I'm aching all over now – including my teeth. There's so much G-force on this track."

While Mansell was thrilling the early spectators, other drivers were having their own private qualifying battle. Patrese ended up with the second fastest time – 1.9 seconds slower than his team-mate – with Senna 2.74 seconds adrift in third place, and Schumacher in fourth.

The following day started out damp and ended up wet. Mansell was once again the fastest but as the weather deteriorated it restricted the drivers and none of the times made any difference to the grid. Patrese escaped unhurt from a nasty shunt, and the young English driver Damon Hill qualified for his first Grand Prix.

On race day not even the threat of rain could keep the fans away, as a crowd of 150,000 spectators gathered to cheer Mansell on. And he didn't let them down. In the warm-up he re-confirmed his position as favourite – the FW14B was running beautifully and with Mansell driving it on his home track, the Williams team were looking invincible.

On the green light he made his only mistake of the weekend, as he failed to get the dream start he had hoped for – too much wheel spin from Mansell enabled Patrese to over-take as they reached the first corner. But Mansell wasn't going to allow his team-mate to steal the show, and as they came out of Copse, sheer speed and determination gave him back the lead.

Mansell wasn't threatened again. He drove a magnificent race, breaking his own lap record on an number of occasions and building up such a commanding advantage that none of the other drivers even contemplated getting near him. After 2 laps he had a 5 second lead, which became 10 seconds after four laps, 17 seconds after 8 and a remarkable 20 seconds by the end of the 10th lap.

He was to maintain this lead over Patrese until the 30th lap when he entered the pits for new tyres. It wasn't his quickest change of the season, but he still managed to return to the track with an 8 second lead, which again became unassailable before too long. Ten seconds after the 32nd lap became 25 seconds by the 50th.

The most intriguing battle was behind Mansell, where Martin Brundle was engaged in a fierce fight for third with Ayrton Senna. The world champion eventually got past him on the 52nd lap only to be struck down almost immediately with engine trouble, allowing Brundle to record a magnificent 3rd.

As Mansell took the flag 39 seconds clear of Patrese, there were scenes of rejoicing the likes of which Silverstone has never witnessed before and, for safety reasons, is unlikely to witness again. Thousands of his supporters broke on to the pit-straight and mobbed his car. In doing so, one fan was run-over, and though he was thankfully uninjured (Mansell had slowed right down) the fans were in very real danger from the rest of the cars who were still finishing at high speeds.

But nothing was going to spoil the day of unashamed British rejoicing. They engulfed Mansell's car, wrestled him from the cockpit and then held him aloft in the fashion reserved for true sporting heroes. Though he had to be rescued by police and race marshals, he didn't mind being mobbed and was quick to dedicate the victory to his supporters.

"This is the best crowd in the world," he said. "And if some people get over excited, that is okay as this is a great day for British motor racing." He said the crowd's support was so intense that he felt them blowing him down the straight, supplying him with an extra "300 revs", while at the same time blowing against the other cars.

It was a faultless performance in front of his home crowd. Mansell finished in a time two minutes quicker than his Silverstone victory the year before, crushing all the opposition in a truly absolute fashion. In doing so he recorded his 28th formula one victory and broke Jackie Stewart's British record of Grand Prix wins. Again he refused to talk about winning the championship, but it was now just a matter of when he would win it, and not if. ■

The British Grand Prix
Silverstone is Nigel's adopted home and his fans were there in their thousands to see their hero. Nigel didn't disappoint them, breaking track records every time he left the pits.

The British Grand Prix

The Williams-Renault team were in their element at Silverstone. While Nigel (above) bore the pressures of his fans and the media, the team worked to ensure his car was set up to perfection every time he sat in it (below and right).

CAMEL
Labatt's
elf
5
EAGLE
GOODYEAR
Canon
Bull.
FRED PERRY

1992

British Grand Prix Results

12 July • 59 laps, 191.573 miles

Starting Positions

1	N Mansell	2	R Patrese
3	A Senna	4	M Schumacher
5	G Berger	6	M Brundle
7	J Herbert	8	J Alesi
9	M Hakkinen	10	E Comas

Finishing Positions and points

1	N Mansell	GB	Williams-Renault	10
2	R Patrese	Italy	Williams-Renault	6
3	M Brundle	GB	Benetton-Ford	4
4	M Schumacher	Germany	Benetton-Ford	3
5	G Berger	Austria	McLaren-Honda	2
6	M Hakkinen	Finland	Lotus-Ford	1

1992 Driver's Championship to date and points

1	N Mansell	76	2	R Patrese	40
3	M Schumacher	29	4	G Berger	20
5	A Senna	18	6	M Brundle	13
7	J Alesi	11	8	M Hakkinen	5
8	M Alboreto	5	10	A de Cesaris	4

1992 Constructor's Championship to date and points

1	Williams-Renault	116
2	Benetton-Ford	42
3	McLaren-Honda	38
4	Ferrari	13
5	Lotus-Ford	7
6	Footwork-Mugen	5

Fastest Lap

Mansell 1:22.539 (141.633 mph)

The British Grand Prix
No one could top Nigel Mansell all weekend. From qualifying (top left and top right) through to the race itself (left), Nigel was the fastest. But for Britain, the slowest was also good news. Williams' test driver Damon Hill fought his recalcitrant Brabham into 26th on the grid and then finished his first race as the last classified runner.

The British Grand Prix

On lap one, Nigel opened a gap of 2 seconds over Patrese (left) on his way to a brilliant win. On a hot summer's afternoon, nothing delighted the crowd more (below), after Saturday's wet conditions (above and right).

Canon
Canon
Canon
RENAULT
elf
Canon
Labatt's
Labatt's
Labatt's
RENAULT
elf
5
GOODYEAR
GOODYEAR
Canon
Canon

The British Grand Prix

As Nigel holds his winners trophy aloft (left) and celebrates with Patrese and Brundle (above) the 150,000 strong crowd go wild (below). Nigel returns their delighted appreciation (right) before celebrating his 28th win in quieter fashion with his wife Rosanne (far right).

Labatt's
RENAULT
elf
CHAMPION
BRITISH
DENIM
Mobil
11

1992

The German Grand Prix

Throughout the 1992 Formula One season, Nigel Mansell always tried to play down any advantage the Williams' drivers enjoyed over their rivals. The Williams-Renault partnership had indeed produced a fabulous car, and Mansell has always been the first to sing its praise, but he also maintained that it does not give him and his fellow driver, Riccardo Patrese, the ascendancy some people believe.

Indeed, this opinion was shared by none other than Ron Dennis, head of the rival McLaren-Honda team. He witnessed Mansell putting in another superb display while qualifying in pole position for the German Grand Prix, and was generous in his praise.

"He is driving brilliantly," he said, "but his is also a very powerful car, too. Indeed, it's like a stallion, and Mansell has been quite brilliant at riding it. I think a lot of people underestimated his driving ability."

During the Friday sessions Mansell lapped in a time two seconds quicker than his nearest rival, Ayrton Senna, and the following day he looked even better. Conditions for qualifying weren't ideal; work carried out on the Hockenheim circuit to try and slow it down had led to a lot more bumps and this resulted in a large number of drivers spinning off. To get in a good time it was important to go out as early as possible in each session to try and avoid traffic and any debris left on the track.

On Saturday morning, Mansell's lapping was even more impressive and far quicker than on the Friday. His time of 1 minute 37.808 seconds was over a second up on his previous best, and only Patrese came anywhere near it. But he never really threatened, and the grid followed the same old pattern of Mansell in pole, with Patrese second and the McLarens of Senna and Berger on the second row.

Once again Mansell suffered too much wheel-spin as the race started and this allowed Patrese to take a temporary lead. The wheel-spin also caused slight problems with his gear-change and Mansell was rather fortunate to reach the first bend with only Patrese ahead of him.

But on the following straight Mansell restored the usual order as he passed Patrese and started to build himself a lead. Patrese in turn was comfortably ahead of Senna, while the German crowd's obvious favourite, Michael Schumacher, was trying to wrestle fourth place from Gerhard Berger.

On lap 14, however, Mansell decided to pit for some new tyres, as a warning light signalled a puncture. In doing so he lost the lead to Patrese, with Ayrton Senna also moving in front of him. An old-fashioned tussle with his great rival then ensued, with Senna using all his experience and knowledge to hold Mansell at bay for several laps.

On lap 19 Mansell made his move. As the two cars approached the chicane, Senna took the first bend in ordinary fashion, but Mansell ploughed straight across it re-emerging on the other side in a cloud of dust. The split second saved by the risky manoeuvre enabled him to overtake the Brazilian on the straight, and when Patrese pitted for new tyres at the end of the lap, Mansell was back in the lead.

It was a lead he was to maintain until the end of the race, and he took the chequered flag 4.5 seconds clear of Ayrton Senna. Patrese found himself fourth after his tyre change and

though he managed to pass Schumacher, his attempts to over-take Senna resulted in him spinning off on the last lap. Schumacher, therefore, finished in third place to the delight of the 125,000 strong crowd.

Nigel Mansell had done it again. It was his eighth victory of the season, equalling the record held by Ayrton Senna, and the ten points he secured also meant that if he was to win the next Grand Prix, in Hungary, then he would also win the Championship. But still he refused to acknowledge that the title was his.

"You weren't in Australia in 1986," he said when asked about the championship being his. "It's closer but I will not say anything about it." He was one victory away from the title and, sensibly, he was still taking nothing for granted." ■

The German Grand Prix

Two seconds faster than Patrese in qualifying (right), Nigel and Frank Williams check the cars performance on the banks of computer telemetry systems in the garages (above).

Runden Start Stop
Mobil 1

RENAULT
elf
Bull

RENAULT
elf
canon
Labatt's
Bull
5

The German Grand Prix

(Top left) The lights turn to green and the cars accelerate away, reaching over 100 mph in under 5 seconds. Nigel (above) instantly takes the lead and pulls away from the rest. (Left) The car at rest with the Williams race team and also as Mansell is used to it, closer to 200mph. (Right) Mansell tears through Hockenheim's giant stadium section.

The German Grand Prix

(Above) Following his tyre-stop Nigel prepares to pass Senna to regain his lead. (Left) Martin Brundle holds off Ivan Capelli's Ferrari on his way to 4th, while Benetton team mate Schumacher (below) finishes 3rd. (Right) Victory number eight in 1992 for Britain's most successful race winner ever.

German Grand Prix Results

26 July • 45 laps, 190.599 miles

Starting Positions

1	N Mansell	2	R Patrese
3	A Senna	4	G Berger
5	J Alesi	6	N Schumacher
7	E Comas	8	T Boutsen
9	M Brundle	10	K Wendlinger

Finishing Positions and points

1	N Mansell	GB	Williams-Renault	10
2	A Senna	Brazil	McLaren-Honda	6
3	M Schumacher	Germany	Benetton-Ford	4
4	M Brundle	GB	Benetton-Ford	3
5	J Alesi	France	Ferrari	2
6	E Comas	France	Ligier-Renault	1

1992 Driver's Championship to date and points

1	N Mansell	86	2	R Patrese	40
3	M Schumacher	33	4	A Senna	24
5	G Berger	20	6	M Brundle	16
7	J Alesi	13	8	M Hakkinen	5
9	M Alboreto	5	10	A de Cesaris	4
10	E Comas	4			

1992 Constructor's Championship to date and points

1	Williams-Renault	126
2	Benetton-Ford	49
3	McLaren-Honda	44
4	Ferrari	15
5	Lotus-Ford	7
6	Footwork-Mugen	5

Fastest Lap

Patrese 1:41.591 (150.060 mph)

Nottingham Forest...

One of the may responsibilities of any top sporting personality is to justify the vast sums of money that companies are prepared to pay in sponsorship and product endorsement. Being successful is the best way of ensuring that your sponsors money is well spent, as success breeds exposure, and exposure is obviously what the sponsors are after.

As you would expect, the overheads for a successful Formula One team are extremely high, despite the fact that most of them are given free engines, free fuel and free tyres, by manufacturers who want to be associated with Grand Prix racing at the highest level.

Williams have a 200-strong staff working on their team all year round, and thirty five of these will travel to each of the Grand Prix races. Then there are the costs for transporting the team and cars to sixteen venues world wide, the staff wages, including those of the drivers, the cost of renting tracks for testing, hiring security personnel – the list goes on. All in all, Williams estimate they run to a budget of about £20 million per year, most of which comes from sponsorship.

One of Mansell's duties, therefore, was to help promote the sponsors, and this often means more than just allowing a certain amount of branding on the car or driver's suit. An example of this was when he visited the City Ground to help promote Labatt's, who are a major sponsor of the Williams team and Nottingham Forest Football Club. ■

Mansell appears on behalf of sponsors Labatt's at the City Ground with the Nottingham Forest football team (above), and children Leo and Greg (bottom left and top right).

SHIPSTONES Fine Beers
Labatt's
SHIPSTONES
GOODYEAR
EAGLE

Labatt's
Canon
RENAULT
elf
CHAMPION
Nigel Mansell

Beers SHIPSTONES
Labatt's
elf
GOODYEAR

GATE 3
SHIPSTONES

1992

The Hungarian Grand Prix

Nigel Mansell was finally in sight of what he had been dreaming of for nearly thirty years. For the second time in his career, he was one race away from the being World Champion and he knew exactly what was required of him. After so many commanding performances in the season to date, surely it was possible for him to end all the speculation about his ability and secure the title, despite the fact that there were still five Grand Prix races remaining.

In 1986 in Adelaide, third place would have been enough to guarantee him the Championship. At the Hungarian Grand Prix on the dusty Hungaroring track, it depended on where he finished in relation to his main rivals, Riccardo Patrese and Michael Schumacher. These two drivers still had a very remote chance of overtaking his points total, so the only way of making certain was by gaining the maximum ten points.

Amid certain speculation as to the legality of certain fuels, most of the teams had opted to use canisters of commercial petrol. Some observers felt that the Williams' cars had an unfair advantage due to the superiority of Elf, but after the first day of qualifying they were proved ill-informed – the two Williams cars were still out in front. This time, however, it was Patrese who set the pace in the sweltering heat with a lap time a tenth of a second ahead of Mansell, and nearly a second ahead of Senna's McLaren.

The temperatures dropped slightly on the Saturday morning, but the positions remained the same. In the afternoon, the atmosphere grew more and more tense as each of the drivers attempted to get clear runs. Berger lost control of his car and caused a number of other cars to spin off the track, including Mansell who collided with the guardrail.

But none of this effected the earlier grid positions. The two Williams were again on the front row, with Patrese gaining his first pole position of the season, followed by Senna, Schumacher and a troubled Berger. Mansell was unhappy with not gaining pole, but knew that he was still in a good enough position to win. After all, he won the Hungarian Grand prix in 1989, despite being twelfth on the grid.

As the lights flicked green, both the Williams got away well. Mansell attempted to get ahead of this team-mate, but as they came to the first turn Patrese kept his line and pushed him wide. This also allowed Senna and Berger to get past him, this time taking the outside line.

It was a poor start by Mansell's standards and with the two McLarens ahead of him, he knew his team-mate would be able to build up a lead. And this he duly did – after four laps he was 6.1 seconds clear. The order stayed the same until the eighth lap, when Mansell moved ahead of Berger.

By lap 21 Patrese was 23 seconds clear, while Mansell was having a torrid time trying to overtake Senna. The Brazilian is the best in the world at holding his line and he made it impossible for Mansell to pass on such a tight track. Indeed, it forced Mansell into making an error, and on lap 31 Berger moved up into the third. But it only lasted three laps, as Mansell managed to squeeze through an impossible gap to re-take third place.

If things stood as they were then Mansell was going to have to wait at least another two weeks before he could claim the title. But on lap 39 it all changed. Patrese spun out of a corner and hit a kerb. He rejoined the race in seventh place, but retired soon after. With his main rival gone, all Mansell needed to do was stay in second and pick up the six points. He was in no great rush and was more than happy to allow Senna to build up a comfortable lead.

It should have been plain sailing for the Williams driver from then on, but on lap 55, his team could see he had a problem – a slow puncture – which Mansell had been unaware of because the warning light was not functioning. Surely Mansell was not going to be the victim of more cruel luck.

On lap 61 the pit called him in after an swift tyre change he rejoined the race in sixth place. With a new set of tyres it didn't take him long to pass those immediately in front of him and regain second place, especially after Schumacher spun into a sand trap on lap 64.

By lap 69, Mansell was back in second and this was how it stayed. It had been a tough, uncompromising race, which had never really gone his way. But he remained calm, kept his concentration and as he finished the 77th lap the chequered flag signalled a new World Champion. Nothing and nobody could take that from him now.

Naturally, Mansell was overcome with joy as he greeted his wife and the Williams team. "I've been close so many times before and wondered whether it might not feel that good when I eventually got the Championship, but I can tell you, its the most fantastic, unbelievable feeling of my life. All the effort, all the heartache is now worthwhile," he said.

"I must dedicate this championship to all those who believed in me and supported me over the years, the marvellous fans, especially those in Britain, who persuaded me I shouldn't retire, and to everyone connected with the team who have put in such a fabulous effort to make this day possible."

And as usual, he took the opportunity to thank his wife Roseanne, who has been by his side through thick-and-thin. "She has given me the support and strength when I've needed it."

Red 5 was the new Formula One World Champion. He had won it comprehensively and in style. Not for 21 years has the World Championship been settled so early in the season and he could now take his deserved place amongst the other great drivers. n

(Above) Mansell came to Hungary knowing he could win the World Championship. Suddenly, the pressure on him was immense.

1992

The Hungarian Grand Prix
(Far left) With the Championship in sight, Mansell hesitates at the start with Riccardo Patrese and Ayrton Senna slotting into the lead. (Above) Another puncture leaves Mansell fighting desperately with Berger and Brundle for the third place he needs for the title. (Left) Senna goes into the pits for fresh tyres on his way to victory, and Nigel's 2nd place (below) is enough to ensure that he is the 1992 World Champion.

Nigel Mansell becomes World Champion and finally achieves his life's ambition after thirteen years and 176 Grand Prix races.

canon
CAMEL
Labatt's
GOODYEAR
canon
elf
RENAULT
Labatt's
canon

The Hungarian Grand Prix

(Above) Mansell pushes his oil covered car to that elusive Championship win. (Below) The years of struggle are over, the dream realised, World Champion Nigel Mansell with Ayrton Senna and Gerhard Berger (right) lets his emotions show as he becomes the World's Number One.

Hungarian Grand Prix Results

16 August • 77 laps, 189.85 miles

Starting Positions

1	R Patrese	2	N Mansell
3	A Senna	4	M Schumacher
5	G Berger	6	M Brundle
7	M Alboreto	8	T Boutsen
9	J Alesi	10	I Capelli

Finishing Positions and points

1	A Senna	Brazil	McLaren-Honda	10
2	N Mansell	GB	Williams-Renault	6
3	G Berger	Austria	McLaren-Honda	4
4	M Hakkinen	Finland	Lotus	3
5	M Brundle	GB	Benetton-Ford	2
6	I Capelli	Italy	Ferrari	1

1992 Driver's Championship to date and points

1	N Mansell	92	2	R Patrese	40
3	A Senna	34	4	M Schumacher	33
5	G Berger	24	6	M Brundle	18
7	J Alesi	13	8	M Hakkinen	8
9	M Alboreto	5	10	A de Cesaris	4
10	E Comas	4			

1992 Constructor's Championship to date and points

1	Williams-Renault	132
2	McLaren-Honda	58
3	Benetton-Ford	51
4	Ferrari	16
5	Lotus-Ford	10
6	Footwork-Mugen	5

Fastest Lap

Mansell 1:18.308 (113.349 mph)

1992

The Belgian Grand Prix

Mansell was clearly in a confident mood as he arrived at the tree-lined Spa-Francorchamps circuit for the Belgium Grand Prix, despite a certain amount of speculation regarding his future at Williams. Rumour had it that Williams had been approached by Ayrton Senna, who was then informed that they had already offered a contract to Alain Prost.

So where did this leave the World Champion, and was it going to effect him over the next few days racing? "I have nothing to prove," said a relaxed Mansell, "A huge weight has been taken from my shoulders. I have achieved what I set out to do. I am determined as ever to drive fast and well." Regarding his future at Williams, Mansell was keeping quiet. He obviously had more pressing things on his mind and was content just to get on with the task in hand.

Conditions always play a major part in Belgium, as the weather has the cruel knack of being able to completely change in the space of a short time. On the first day of qualifying, Mansell was again in superb form, ending the session 2.19 seconds ahead of Senna. Michael Schumacher – who had taken a nasty spin earlier in the day – was third on the grid and Patrese fourth. Thankfully Eric Comas, who was taken to Liege for a brain scan after a bad crash earlier in the day, was declared fit.

During Friday night the weather closed in, and throughout the Saturday morning session it rained continuously. There was little chance that any one was going to improve on their Friday times, but still they tried. First out was Berger, and he spun badly. He was followed by Pierluigi Martini, who spun on exactly the same part of the track. And then the officials stopped the session. It was the same in the afternoon, and the grid from the Friday was how it stood for the race.

The warm-up confirmed Mansell's superiority, but surprisingly the young Schumacher was the next fastest. As the cars completed the parade lap, the weather again started to change. It had been fine during the morning so most of the cars had gone with slick tyres, but as they waited for the green light it became obvious they would have to be changed.

Though Senna got the better start than Mansell, and led for the first couple of laps, it wasn't long before the current World Champion

cruised past the man he deposed of the title. And then it was into the pits for a tyre change, with all the other cars gradually following suit. All, that is, except for Senna: he realised he had to try something different if he was going to have any chance of challenging the Williams drivers. He therefore gambled on the conditions improving fairly rapidly.

But by lap 14 Senna had no choice but to change to wets, and as he pitted, Mansell again took the lead. On lap 30 Michael Schumacher noticed the blisters on his team-mate's tyres and decided to return to slicks. It was an inspired decision taken at exactly the right moment. He was followed by Brundle and then it was the turn of the Williams drivers, though Mansell had to wait a lap before he could go in.

"I wanted to come in for the second tyre stop, but the team told me to wait so that Riccardo could come in first and I respected that," Mansell commented after the race.

While the two Williams drivers were changing, Schumacher was flying round, and by lap 34, when all the stops had been completed, he had a 6 second lead from Mansell, who was followed by Patrese and Brundle, with Senna in sixth.

On equal tyres, Mansell gradually began to close the gap on Schumacher, and at one stage he was within three seconds of the German. But then he began to lose power, the result of some exhaust problems down one side of the car. There was no way he was going to catch Schumacher now and the Benetton driver continued his brilliant drive to record his first Formula One victory, while Mansell held off the challenge of Patrese and Brundle to take second.

"I was looking forward to the last seven laps," the World Champion explained during the post-race press conference, "but then the exhaust fell off the car and I lost something like 1400 revs on the straight, which slowed me down by about five seconds every lap."

However, Mansell was still in jubilant mood as the result had given the Williams-Renault team the Constructor's World Championship. "I was happy to finish and I am delighted for the whole team who really deserve this victory," he concluded. ■

The Belgian Grand Prix
The new World Champion is released from the pressures of the title race and (top left) a relaxed and confident Mansell sweeps to pole position once again, this time around the Spa-Francorchamps circuit.

The Belgian Grand Prix

(Above and left) Ayrton Senna gets the jump at the start but his lead is short lived as Mansell (right) passes him on the second lap. But it is the young German, Michael Schumacher, who finds himself in the lead after the tyre stops, as he sweeps in to Eau Rouge (below).

Canon
Labatt's
RENAULT
elf
5

The Belgian Grand Prix

(Below) Nigel Mansell ahead of his team mate Patrese and the Benetton duo early on in the wet. (Above and left) Mansell and Schumacher strike sparks as conditions improve and the race picks up, but a misfire halted Mansell's charge, allowing the 23 year old to claim his first victory (right) exactly one year after starting his Formula One career.

Belgian Grand Prix Results

30th August • 44 laps, 190.671 miles

Starting Positions

1	N Mansell	2	A Senna
3	M Schumacher	4	R Patrese
5	J Alesi	6	G Berger
7	T Boutsen	8	M Hakkinen
9	M Brundle	10	J Herbert

Finishing Positions and points

1	M Schumacher	Germany	Benetton-Ford	10
2	N Mansell	GB	Williams-Renault	6
3	R Patrese	Italy	Williams-Renault	4
4	M Brundle	GB	Benetton-Ford	3
5	A Senna	Brazil	McLaren-Honda	2
6	M Hakkinen	Finland	Lotus-Ford	1

1992 Driver's Championship to date and points

1	N Mansell	98	2	R Patrese	44
3	M Schumacher	43	4	A Senna	36
5	G Berger	24	6	M Brundle	21
7	J Alesi	13	8	M Hakkinen	9
9	M Alboreto	5	10	A de Cesaris	4
10	E Comas	4			

1992 Constructor's Championship to date and points

1	Williams-Renault	142
2	Benneton-Ford	64
3	McLaren-Honda	60
4	Ferrari	16
5	Lotus-Ford	11
6	Footwork-Mugen	5

Fastest Lap

Schumacher 1:53.791 (137.097 mph)

1992

The Italian Grand Prix

The world of Formula One has always been shrouded in secrecy and covert dealings. It is rife with furtive arrangements, back-stabbing accusations and clandestine negotiations. This has never been more apparent than during the build-up to the Italian Grand Prix at Monza, where all the talk and gossip was centred around Nigel Mansell's future in Grand Prix racing.

It was hardly the ideal build up for the reigning World Champion. Despite having secured Williams their first driver's title for five years, Mansell was still unsure as to his future, and the speculation and rumours that filtered through the pits could not have helped his preparation.

However, it is a testament to Mansell's professionalism as a driver, that he managed to put all the chaos and conjecture to the back of his mind as he roared home to record the 28th pole position of his

career. Ayrton Senna accompanied him on the front row, while Jean Alesi, despite having two accidents, gave the tifosi something to cheer when he qualified third in his Ferrari.

Between the racing, Mansell's day was punctuated by meetings with team bosses, fuel company executives and Formula One officials. But still he was unable to give any indication as to his future, much to the dismay of the growing ranks of impatient journalists.

But on the day of the race, and only hours before the start, Mansell called a press conference and, to the surprise of everyone, announced his retirement. Negotiations with Williams had quite simply broken down. He was dissatisfied with the way he had been treated, and felt there was no alternative but to withdraw from Formula One racing at the end of the season, despite a last minute attempt by a Williams official to make him change his mind.

There were a number of reasons he gave for his decision – the fact that Alain Prost had already struck a deal with Williams for 1993 without his knowledge, that he was told he would have to take a 50 per cent cut in remuneration, and that he thought he already had an agreement with Williams for 1993, are just a few. And whether or not these were justified, there is no disguising the fact that he did not receive the respect due to a World Champion.

As he said at the press conference, "To say that I have been badly treated, I think, is a gross understatement." More than a few of those present had to agree with him.

Amid all this confusion and ill-feeling there was also another round of the World Championship to be settled. It started in a sensational fashion, with Mansell leading and Alesi sending the crowd wild as he momentarily captured second place from Senna. But the McLaren driver soon cut him out, and by the end of the second lap Patrese had joined his team-mate at the front with Senna and Alesi a few seconds behind.

On lap 20 the lead changed, as Mansell, 12 seconds in front, slowed down to let his Italian team-mate through. The Williams pair then entertained the crowds to some exhibition driving, before the World Champion was forced to retire with a jammed gearbox on the 42nd lap.

With Mansell gone, it looked as if Patrese was going to be the first home driver to win the Italian Grand Prix since 1966. But on lap 48 he started to experience problems with his suspension and he could only finish fifth. Senna made the most of the Williams driver's misfortune to secure an unlikely victory, his third of the season, with Martin Brundle recording his best ever finish in second, and his team-mate Michael Schumacher in third.

It had been an eventful couple of days, with contractual disputes unfortunately receiving more attention than the racing. It was not a very good week all-round for Mansell and the Williams team, and one could only wait to see if another chapter in their worsening relations was about to unfold. ■

MARELLI
MARELLI
MARELLI
elf
5
Canon
Bull

MARELLI
MARELLI
MARELLI
MARELLI
GOODYEAR
Marlboro
Labatts

(Above) Patrese takes Senna for 2nd place before passing Mansell (below and right) for the lead. Nigel's day was not a happy one (below), retiring from the race while Senna (top right) went on to win, although he found little cheer (top far right), with his career's future, like Mansell's, in doubt.

Italian Grand Prix Results

13 September • 53 laps, 191.009 miles

Starting Positions

1	N Mansell	2	A Senna
3	J Alesi	4	R Patrese
5	G Berger	6	M Schumacher
7	I Capelli	8	T Boutsen
9	M Brundle	10	B Gachot

Finishing Positions and points

1	A Senna	Brazil	McLaren-Honda	10
2	M Brundle	GB	Benetton-Ford	6
3	M Schumacher	Germany	Benetton-Ford	4
4	G Berger	Austria	McLaren-Honda	3
5	R Patrese	Italy	Williams-Renault	2
6	A de Cesaris	Italy	Tyrell-Ilmor	1

1992 Driver's Championship to date and points

1	N Mansell	98	2	M Schumacher	47
3	R Patrese	46	3	A Senna	46
5	G Berger	27	5	M Brundle	27
7	J Alesi	13	8	M Hakkinen	9
9	M Alboreto	5	9	A de Cesaris	5

1992 Constructor's Championship to date and points

1	Williams-Renault	144
2	Benetton-Ford	74
3	McLaren-Honda	73
4	Ferrari	16
5	Lotus-Ford	11
6	Footwork-Mugen	5
	Tyrell-Ilmor	5

Fastest Lap

Mansell 1:26.119 (150.655 mph)

1992

The Final Lap...

At the time of writing this book, there was no clear indication of exactly what lay ahead for Nigel Mansell. He had declared his intention of retiring from Formula One at the end of the 1992 season, but apart from that he had said little else about his future plans.

Mansell has always had a strong belief in his own abilities, when others have often doubted his temperament and skill, and perhaps this accounts for his poor track record in team relations. In hindsight, maybe some of his past team managers should have given him the number one spot, or at least made more of an effort to supply him with a reliable car!

Formula One racing has never been renowned for its loyalty. To succeed, it helps to be arrogant, manipulative and cunning, as well as devoid of any sentiment. It takes an emotionally hard character to ignore the political scheming and petty jealousies that surround most of the teams, and perhaps Mansell has had difficulty in shrugging this off.

Though he is obviously a perfectionist, Mansell is also a very down to earth character with an inherent sense of fair-play. During the press conference at which he announced his retirement, he said, "Any relationship between a driver and a Formula One team is vital for success, and partly dependent on money because it defines how seriously the team and its backers take the driver.

"But those who know me well, understand the importance of the human side, and the mutual trust and good will and integrity and fair play that are the basis of all human relationships.

"Looking back, I feel the relationship between me and the Williams team started to break down in Hungary. A deal was agreed with Frank before the race, in front of a witness, and I have to say that at the time I felt very good about racing again in 1993."

Three days later, a Williams official phoned Mansell to tell him that the deal was off, and that he would have to accept a massive reduction in remuneration if he wanted a Williams seat the following season. It is exactly this sort of underhand treatment that Mansell found so hard to ignore, and ultimately it was this lack of loyalty, rather than the financial situation, which led to the announcement of his retirement.

The whole charade surrounding Nigel Mansell did little to enhance the image of the Williams team, in an age when the world economic recession was doing Formula One no favours. Mansell was the World Champion and yet it appeared that this accolade stood for nothing!

During the press conference, Mansell made it clear that he did not want to give up racing altogether. Rumour had it that he was already considering a very attractive offer to take a step across the Atlantic and drive Indy Cars for the Newman-Haas team. If he does decide to keep on driving, this would be the obvious move for him to make.

But many a Grand Prix fan felt the saga of Mansell's career in Formula One had still to run its full course. After all, this wasn't the first time he had announced his retirement, and the history of on-off deals within the sport certainly made this a possibility. It is also within his competitive nature to want to defend his title, and one suspected we were in store for one or two more episodes of the Nigel Mansell soap opera.

If Mansell does retire, then he will be sorely missed by his army of followers, for there is no doubting he is one of the finest racers to grace a circuit. However, in the uncertain world of Formula One, one cannot be sure of anything, and if he does decide to race again, there will be more than a few fans waiting to hear Il Leone roar. ■

 Mansell wins the Portuguese Grand Prix making it a record 9 wins in a Championship.

OS
ER'S
BR
MANSE
Canon
Canon
Canon